LIVING
THE LIFE
GOD HAS
PLANNED

A Guide to
Knowing
God's Will

Bill Thrasher

Mo
C

© 2001 by
DR. WILLIAM D. THRASHER

All rights reserved. No part of this book may be reproduced in any
form without permission in writing from the publisher, except in the
case of brief quotations embodied in critical articles or reviews.

All Scripture quotations are taken from the *New American Standard
Bible®*, © Copyright The Lockman Foundation 1960, 1962, 1963,
1968, 1971, 1972, 1973, 1975, 1977, 1995. Used by permission.

Library of Congress Cataloging-in-Publication Data
Thrasher, Bill, 1952-
   Living the life God has planned : a guide to knowing God's will /
Bill Thrasher.
      p. cm.
   Includes bibliographical references.
   ISBN 0-8024-3699-4
   1. Christian life. 2. God—Will. I. Title.

BV4501.3 .T48 2001
248.4—dc21

00-048056

1 3 5 7 9 10 8 6 4 2

Printed in the United States of America

Among the numerous articles and books I have read on this topic of discovering God's will, Dr. Bill Thrasher's book stands out as one of the best. Why? He places the quest to know God's will into biblical perspective. God wants us to know His will, but He wants to provide something much more valuable than a road map. He offers Himself through His Son Jesus Christ. In this gem of a book the reader will see that those who become intimate with the Shepherd are the ones who most clearly hear His voice.

Lyle Dorsett
Professor of Educational Ministries & Evangelism
Wheaton College

Living the Life God Has Planned is a book for everyone. Gender and age exclude no one who desires to find, follow, and finish God's plan for their life (Eph. 2:10). Since the highest end of God's will is God Himself, relationship with God through His Son and by His Spirit is the only way to "prove what is that good, and acceptable, and perfect, will of God" (Rom. 12:2).

My dear friend, Dr. Bill Thrasher, expounds and exemplifies both doctrine and delight of knowing and doing God's will in daily life. In a day of confusion, purposelessness, and frustration in the world—and, alas, in the church as well—we have in this book a clear guide for all of us. Thank you, Bill Thrasher, for an excellent treatment of a subject that demands the attention of all who desire to live for the glory of God alone. I pray that this book will bless the multitudes who seek God's best for their lives.

Stephen F. Olford
Founder & Senior Lecturer
The Stephen Olford Center for Biblical Preaching

To the Lord Jesus Christ,
whose beautiful attributes unlock the
door to the experience of His will.

Contents

SECTION THREE:
KNOWING GOD'S CHARACTER
IN ORDER TO DISCERN HIS WILL

SECTION FOUR:
KNOWING GOD'S DESIRE FOR YOU

Foreword

G et a life!" is street talk for getting a grip on the right perspective. In fact, if we stop to think about it we spend most of our lives trying to do just that . . . getting a life. Billions of dollars are spent annually on trying to figure it all out. Counselors, books, talk shows, over-coffee advice and late night personal planning sessions exhaust us as we toss and turn alone in darkened bedrooms.

And it's no wonder we are concerned. Trying to unravel the complexities of relationships, the difference between reality and fantasy in our plans and dreams, the establishment of boundaries in the pursuit of our desires, and the right mix of values, money and stuff make figuring life out a tough job. Add to the challenge the unpredictable and daunting task of trying to get a handle on our inner selves and you have a lifelong pursuit of an illusive dream. And, if you happen to be one of the few blessed ones to semmingly have it "all together," look out. Lurking around the corner just may be an unscheduled shock that will throw it all up in the air again, sending you back to square one.

Getting life right is a critically important matter. Those who opt for a resignation to the passive fatalism of the "whatever will be, will be" approach to life find that a life left to the severe winds of chance usually suffers the damage of wasted opportunities and regret.

Thankfully, my friend and colleague Bill Thrasher has put his pen to the daunting task of helping us put all of life in a meaningful and productive perspective. Not because he personally has all the answers. No one could be that presumptive. But because he knows the One who is qualified to show us the way.

In this insightful and realistically practical book, Bill simply takes us to the life perspectives of the God who designed it all in the first place. And he does it clearly, convincingly, and relevantly. This is no "pie in the sky" treatment of the vast complexities of our existence. This is down to earth reality therapy from the best Counselor in the universe.

Soon into the book you will know why he is a favorite professor in our Moody Graduate School. His clarity and convictingly straightforward style never overshadow his compassionate spirit and personal interest in leading those who will listen to God's best. He consistently reminds me of the qualities of Jesus who, as John noted, was "full of grace and truth" (John 1:14). You will be blessed by both of these qualities as your life is nurtured into a meaningful perspective through the pages of this book.

JOSEPH M. STOWELL, PRESIDENT
MOODY BIBLE INSTITUTE

Acknowledgments

I t is a pleasure to acknowledge the loving support of my wife, Penny, who carefully read the manuscript and made helpful suggestions, as well as my three sons, Will, Michael, and David, who provide daily encouragement and joy to my life. I also am indebted to my mother, Carolyn Thrasher, and parents-in-law, Dr. and Mrs. William J. Bauer, for their prayer support.

I am grateful for the opportunity to work with Greg Thornton and Bill Thrasher (anyone with a name like that has to be a good guy), who enabled the project to get started. Bill Soderberg's helpful suggestions and editing helped make the book a reality along with the able editorial assistance of Cheryl Dunlop. I would also like to thank Dawn Culbreth for typing the manuscript.

It has been a privilege to work with wonderful colleagues and so many precious students at the Moody Bible Institute. They have enriched my life in countless ways.

Knowing God's Purpose for Your Life

◆

God's Purpose for Human Existence

T om and Becky left the pastor's office with decid-
edly different ideas running through their minds.
Engaged to be married in a few weeks, they had come
to the pastor's office for premarital counseling at his request, since they had asked him to conduct the marriage ceremony. Becky was already a believer. Everything
Pastor Jenkins said about marriage being ordained by
God and being holy made sense to her. She was beaming.

Tom, on the other hand, was not so excited. In fact
he was deeply troubled. Growing up outside of a
Christian home, he was taught that organized religion
was a foolish and obsolete contrivance for simple
minds. Surely, his teachers at all levels of school had
taught him, man is a product of evolution, of random

chemical and electrical processes developing over millions of years. Hadn't science proved that over and over again?

The two had met at college and fallen in love. When they decided to get married, Tom agreed to become "a churchgoer" to gain the approval of Becky's parents. He decided that Becky was worth putting up with this nuisance, at least until they were married. Later, he would let her go to church if she wanted to, but he would stay at home. Right away, though, his carefully laid plans began to crumble. Many things he heard in church, things that challenged his years of secular education, moved Tom. Many "truths" he had learned were challenged in church in ways he couldn't counter or disagree with.

But he was an engineer by profession. Science was the god of his life. If it couldn't be worked out on a computer or in a laboratory, it wasn't real. The Garden of Eden was a fairy tale. It had to be. "Look at the fossil record," he told himself repeatedly. "Man is descended from crude, simple amoebae, developing over billions of years. Countless generations of life forms demonstrate that truth."

Inside, however, he couldn't reconcile himself to the troubling sense that there must be more to life than being an accidental byproduct of certain chemical energy processes. Life must have purpose and meaning. Becky was certainly no accident! And Tom's own life must have some meaning apart from his own impulses. That part of the scientific argument didn't compute.

The scientists just ignored man's inner self because they couldn't see it under a microscope!

It continued to bother Tom that he couldn't fit all the pieces together, and it bothered him more than he would admit that the whole picture seemed to make sense to Becky. But one day he realized, "Science is always coming up with new answers. They can't be far away from answering this one too." After that it bothered him less that Becky's answer still seemed more satisfying than his, but it still haunted him sometimes as he prepared to spend his life with her.

THE MEANING OF LIFE

The age-old question jokingly debated in all entry-level college philosophy courses is "What is the meaning of life?" Not a few unfortunate students have been asked to write short but succinct papers trying to answer this simple but all-encompassing question. But a question that should be asked first is "Does God exist?" If we conclude that there is no God, then we are condemned to the hopeless task of finding meaning in a world that evolutionists readily admit is a product of random accident.

If, on the other hand, we conclude that the world could only have come about as a result of some creative force, a force beyond the imagination of men and their myths, a real and omniscient, omnipresent God, then the search for human meaning goes in an entirely different direction. If we accept the God of the Bible, revealed to us in His holy Scripture and in the world around us that He created, then we may take the question a step further and ask, "What is God like?"

Dr. Howard Hendricks is a renowned seminary professor who has taught Bible study methods to hundreds of men and women preparing for the ministry. Dr. Hendricks was asked one day, "What is the most helpful insight that you have ever learned about studying the Bible?" He replied with this simple answer: "This book teaches me about a Person." We can so easily lose sight of this truth as we study the Bible and learn principles and doctrine, but forget the Person to whom the principles and doctrines point. One can even seek for God's will and forget to seek God.

OUR RELATIONSHIP WITH GOD

The book of Genesis makes it clear that God, despite His limitless power and ability, is a Being with a mind, will, and emotions, much like us. When He created the universe we live in, His crowning accomplishment was to create man in His own image and likeness (Genesis 1:26–27). He created man with the capacity to enjoy His companionship. Such a statement tells us two important things. First, it tells us there were (and are) no other gods like the Creator in the beginning, thus declaring His own uniqueness. Second, He made man with a special care and design, apart from everything else, to be able to enjoy Him in all His perfection. To talk, to walk, to think, to play together. It may be hard for you to imagine going for a walk in the park with God, but that's exactly what Adam and Eve enjoyed.

Of course, the Fall and Adam and Eve's ejection from Eden ruined the harmony of that perfect relationship. A frightful pall of death now surrounds man. Man is stained in his relationship with God since Satan's tempting, for evil cannot coexist with a supremely good and pure God. By seeking to become like God, Adam and Eve violated the one rule they could not break: acknowledging God as Master. Loving, caring, friendly, but still Master.

And yet man was not completely abandoned by God, for God continued to be a presence in the lives of succeeding generations of men and women. Through God's Son, Jesus Christ, who walked among us, we have been given a Savior, a way out from the despair and death that now haunts our lives. During His ministry on earth, God in human form revealed Himself to us and told us how we might know Him and His will for our lives.

THE REVELATION OF GOD IN HUMAN FORM

How does Christ reveal God's nature and will to us? Jesus was talking to a group of "biblical scholars" of His day when He stated that the Scriptures bear witness of Himself (John 5:39). Jesus taught a Bible study on another occasion to His followers and explained how every part of the Bible pointed to Himself (Luke 24:27–

44). Jesus is the climactic revelation of "who God is." Christ is "the radiance of His glory and the exact representation of His nature" (Hebrews 1:3). He is "the image of the invisible God" (Colossians 1:15). He is for this reason called the "Word" (John 1:1, 14). As our words reveal our hearts, so the "Word" revealed or explained the heart and character of God (John 1:18). For this reason, when his disciple Philip asked to see the Father, He replied, "He who has seen Me has seen the Father" (John 14:9). In Jesus, one learns the answer to the question "What is God like?"

God's purpose was not to abandon man in his pride and idolatry but rather to redeem man. First Peter 1:18 states that God has redeemed man from his futile life of independence from God. God's purpose for you is to bring you into a relationship with Himself. *Redeem* is a word that denotes an act of purchase. In New Testament times slaves were purchased from the slave market. The Lord redeemed man from being a slave to his own self-will. The purchase price is one of great and personal cost, for the Lord gave Himself in order to free us (Titus 2:14).

This act of redemption brings to those who believe eternal life, which is defined as an experiential knowledge or relationship with God (John 17:3). To be separated from Him is to experience death (Ephesians 2:1). But God's purpose is that a relationship be developed so that we experience the life that He describes as satisfying and "abundant" (John 6:35; 10:10). Such a relationship necessitates communication.

We could never know God's will apart from His communicating to us through the Bible. We would live in continual darkness apart from the light of His revelation. Although we can see signs of God in nature, it is only through Scripture that we can come to a truer and more complete understanding of Him. God's will for you is to develop your relationship with Him. It is God's will to expose sins such as pride and idolatry in your life.

The first step in knowing God's will and understanding His purpose for you is to trust Jesus Christ as your Savior. In Jesus we see not only that God is holy and demands that sin be punished but also that God is loving and gracious. In Jesus, who took God's punishment for sin for you, you can find a way to escape God's wrath and have peace with God (Romans 5:1).

God is seeking to reveal Himself to you as you seek His will. Let me offer a simple suggestion that I have found to be very helpful. This idea came to me when I set aside a special time to seek the Lord concerning the dryness in my Sunday worship experience. I had ceased to have a sense of anticipation in regard to the Lord's day. It had dwindled to a mere duty.

As I sought the Lord concerning this situation, I walked away from that day with a solemn personal conviction. The conviction was to never have a Lord's day in which I would not seek to share my heart with God. This requires preparation and the enablement of God. I take time during the week to write down the three greatest concerns of my heart, finalizing it on

3 concerns

Saturday night. Then, going into the Lord's day, I lift up these concerns to Him. It may be an upcoming responsibility, an area in which I need direction, a relationship that needs His gracious aid, or a temptation. I write down any insight that God gives in response to the request, and I review it the next week. These sheets of paper are filed away and would be worthless to anybody else. But to me, they are a reminder that my God is a living God who knows my name and address and is willing to be involved in the affairs of my life. God reveals Himself to us in the context of the needs of our hearts. He wants to open His Word to us and show us what He is like as we seek His will.

THE PURPOSE OF OUR REDEMPTION

God has redeemed you to be "zealous for good deeds" (Titus 2:14). He has a place for you. However, all of our good works are to be an overflow of abiding in Him (John 15:5). Our relationship with Him is the primary thing. Our service for Him is secondary. If we aim at the primary thing, we will get the secondary. If we aim at the secondary thing, there is no assurance that we will get it, and for sure we will miss the primary. Jesus was encouraging His followers not to be anxious about food and clothing in Matthew 6:25–34. He concluded His teaching by encouraging them to seek first His kingdom and righteousness and to trust Him with the secondary things of His provision.

I have written to encourage you not to seek God's

will in an anxious spirit but rather to let your pursuit be after the primary thing of building an intimate relationship with God. A person who wants to know God must understand God's purpose for his or her life. God's primary purpose for your life is to build an intimate, loving relationship with Himself. This focused devotion will lead you into the full experience of every facet of His will for you.

◆

Chapter Two

Satan's Scheme to Thwart Man's Harmony with God

A student came to me one day after class and said, "I don't want to ride public transportation anymore." I was puzzled by this unexpected pronouncement. I knew the student didn't have his own car and lived too far away from college and work to walk. My curiosity piqued, I asked him, "Why are giving up on public transportation? Are you buying your own car?"

His reply was not what I expected, but I understood his anguish at once. He said, "Every time I sit down on a bus and don't witness to the person next to me I feel so guilty, *that I have failed God.*"

Was this young man failing to honor the Great Commission every time he sat next to strangers on a bus or train? Was God sending him warning signals to get his act together and present the Gospel, or else? Naturally the Lord wants us to talk about His Word with others, but He doesn't expect us to carry a loud-speaker with us everywhere we go, yelling, "Accept Christ as your Savior today, before it's too late." He provides opportunities for us to be His agents of wit-ness to others when conditions are right for both par-ties. And He doesn't convict us with guilt unless we have genuinely sinned or failed Him in some way.

Satan, on the other hand, doesn't want us to wit-ness, ever. He can place false and oppressive burdens on us that hinder us from experiencing the freedom to love the people around us. His trick is letting us be-lieve the guilt comes from God. Such a view of God leads one to a life of paralyzing fear. Only the truth of God can set us free (John 8:32).

As you seek to understand God's will, you will dis-cern that you are in a spiritual battle. Ultimately your opponent is in the spiritual realm (Ephesians 6:11–12). The Bible teaches that long ago, an angelic crea-ture rebelled against the Creator. This creature is re-ferred to by a variety of names in Scripture; Satan and the devil are probably the best known. _Satan_ means "adversary," and _devil_ means "slanderer." *Because Satan is at war with God, whose supremacy Satan's pride will not accept, he seeks to thwart God by destroying or corrupting His creation, principally man.*

The Scripture warns us not to be ignorant of Sa-tan's schemes (2 Corinthians 2:11). He has a variety of strategies *to separate man from God,* but his most basic one is to distort our understanding of God. If the basic message of the Bible is the answer to the question "What is God like?", it is logical that His adversary would seek to distort this message and slander His character.

SYMPTOMS OF FOLLOWING SATAN

We see Satan using this ploy from the outset in the Garden of Eden. As you read Genesis 3:1–6 you can clearly see his attempt to distort Eve's understanding of God. An examination of this passage reveals the strategy to distort God's faithfulness. The serpent declared God to be a liar by stating "You surely will not die," in contrast to God's statement "You will surely die" (Genesis 3:4; 2:17). *A casual stroll past the neighborhood cemetery will convince you who was telling the truth and who was lying.* He also attacked God's goodness by implying that God wanted Eve's obedience in order to withhold something from her (Genesis 3:5). You and I would never sin unless we thought something good would come out of it. At this point, we are deceived by the lie that seduces man into a life of independence from God for one's own apparent greater benefit.

Satan understands clearly that he must use slightly different tactics to subvert the believer than the unbeliever. He is subtler, simultaneously aware of the message of the Gospel and human weakness. He plays upon our fallen nature, particularly in those persons less filled with the power of God's Word, to trick us into putting our thoughts on ourselves and our failures rather than on God and His ability to work in our lives. Another related temptation, especially for those who *do* know the Word, is thinking that they come closer to meeting God's standards than other believers do. Pride and self-reliance are still some of Satan's most powerful weapons. How can we recognize that other people, or we ourselves, are being distorted by Satan's subtle lies and mind games? Here are a few examples of those temptations.

Symptom #1: Giving God Only External Service

Jesus spoke of this in Matthew 15:8 when He said, "This people honors Me with their lips, but their heart is far away from Me." In Tedd Tripp's book *Shepherding a Child's Heart,* the author reiterates that the goal of parenting is not only to get a child to conform to a correct behavior but to win the child's heart. God, who is a perfect heavenly Father, is not interested in performance Christianity that lacks true heart love. Even in relationship to our giving, God loves a cheerful generosity that arises from the heart as opposed to giving grudgingly (2 Corinthians 9:7).

When confronted with the symptom of external service in our own lives, our response should be to give our hearts unconditionally to God. We must grant Him the freedom to work in us to do His will, not our will. Although He is a good God who desires that we prosper, we must never forget that we are His servants, not the other way around. We judge others by external appearances; God judges us by our hearts. We may not know when others' motives lack integrity, but He does. That's how He measures our real love for Him.

Symptom #2: Believing That God's Commandments Are Burdensome

Most individuals at some time in their spiritual pilgrimage will struggle with this idea. First John 5:3 clearly states that God's commandments are not burdensome. Jesus, the climax of God's revelation of Himself, invited people who were burdened down with religion to experience His yoke. His yoke speaks of His loving control that He said was easy to wear. He declared His load to be light (Matthew 11:28–30).

I argued with God about this verse. I felt that the only way to have a light load was to purpose to live a *superficial* Christian life. But that is not what Jesus said! I used to pad my daily schedule with "Christian stuff" to convince myself that I was serving the Lord and in order to experience that "light burden." But the reality was that I was burdening myself with others' agendas and problems and not always the Lord's. When I recognized that my time was not spent effectively serving the Lord, I changed my daily habits and concentrated on what the Lord wanted me to do in order to serve Him and build my relationship with Him. Almost overnight, my burden became lighter.

I also discovered that it is possible to sense that God's commandments are burdensome when I do God's will with the wrong motivations. I read 1 Peter 5 one day, and it was as if the Spirit of God underlined one of the phrases of verse 2. Peter was telling the elders of the church how to shepherd God's people. One of the three comparisons he gives is not to do it "under compulsion, but voluntarily."

One type of compulsion comes from the Holy Spirit. Paul referred to this in 1 Corinthians 9:16 when he spoke of being "under compulsion" to preach. However, this was not what Peter is talking about in 1 Peter 5:2. He was talking about a *wrongful* compulsion that grieves God's Spirit and chokes one's own heart. It is a compulsion that is not born out of a fear of God but a fear of man.

Have you ever had anyone ask you to do something that you had no desire to do and did not believe that God wanted you to do? Have you ever been afraid to say no in such a situation? I discovered that such a ministry could be very burdensome. If a person is fully surrendered to the Lord, God will give him a "want to" motivation for what He calls him to do. This does not mean that all of God's will is as pleasant as eating pizza and ice cream. It does mean that the motivation comes from within and is not only an external pressure.

I recall one very difficult summer in my own life. The verse of Scripture that got me out of bed each morning was Romans 15:5. This verse teaches that God will give us encouragement and the endurance to keep going. I wrote Romans 15:5 on the top of a sheet of paper and each day noted how God had provided what I needed to enable me to persevere.

There is one great secret to discovering and doing God's will. Paul referred to it in 1 Corinthians 15:10. He said that the secret to His labor was God's gracious motivation and enablement. What kept the apostle going? It was the Lord who gave Him the encouragement and endurance (Romans 15:5). Do you think he felt like being godly every day? Do you think that he even felt like getting up every morning? You can ask him after you get to heaven, and I am sure he will tell you no. The Lord motivated and empowered him (Philippians 2:13).

In order to cast down the thought of God's will being burdensome, we must have a correct perspective of God's loving nature. It requires a complete surrender of ourselves to the Lord, and this will lead to an experience of that which is good, acceptable, and perfect (Romans 12:1–2). Our goals and ambitions need to be fully surrendered to the will of God.

Symptom #3: Considering the Opinion of Men More Important than God's

One morning I awoke and read 1 Corinthians 9. I was struck by verse 19, which said, "For though I am free from all men, I have made myself a slave to all, so that I may win more." What struck me that morning was not the fact that I was to be a servant or slave to all. I knew that I was to do that, even though I am not very good at it. What hit me was the idea of being free from all men. This phrase fascinated me, and I asked God to open up to me the truth of this phrase in my own experience. As I prayed over this for the next year, a few things became clear to me.

What does it mean to be free from man? It means to be free from letting the expectations of others be the lord of your life. It is not that we should not be sensitive to others; in fact, some people are not sensitive enough. It is that we are not to be so sensitive to others' expectations that we become out of tune with the expectations of God. An illustration of this can be seen in the following statement about how some view a pastor. It has been said:

- If he is young, he lacks experience; if his hair is gray, he's too old for the young people.
- If he has several children, he has too many; if he has no children, he's setting a bad example.
- If he preaches from his notes, he has canned sermons and is too dry; if he doesn't use notes, he has not studied and is not deep.
- If he is attentive to the poor people in the church, the members claim he is playing to the grandstand; if he pays attention to the wealthy, he is trying to be an aristocrat.
- If he suggests changes for improvement of the church, he is a dictator; if he makes no suggestions, he is a figurehead.
- If he uses too many illustrations, he neglects the Bible; if he doesn't use enough illustrations, he isn't clear.

- If he condemns wrong, he is cranky; if he doesn't preach against sin, he's a compromiser.
- If he preaches the truth, he's offensive; if he doesn't preach the truth, he's a hypocrite.
- If he fails to please somebody, he's hurting the church and ought to leave; if he tries to please everyone, he is a fool.
- If he preaches about money, he's a money grabber; if he doesn't preach spiritual giving, he is failing to develop the people.
- If he drives an old car, he shames his congregation; if he drives a new car, he is setting his affection on earthly things.
- If he preaches all the time, the people get tired of hearing one man; if he invites guest speakers, he is shirking his responsibility.
- If he receives a large salary, he's mercenary; if he receives only a small salary, well . . . it proves he isn't worth much anyway.   –Author Unknown

To be free from man also means to be free from letting the actions of others be the basis for our joy in the Lord.

Unquestionably, the actions of others will affect us. However, they should not control us or distort our view of God. Their responses may not reflect how God would respond to a given situation.

Remember the woman who broke the vial of very costly perfume and poured it over Jesus' head when He was in Bethany at the home of Simon the leper?

She was scolded for her action, and men declared it to be a wasted effort. Jesus' response was quite different. He declared her action to be a good deed that would be eternally remembered throughout the whole world (Mark 14:3–9).

A prayer that I have prayed, and have seen God graciously answer, is "Lord, when I take steps of obedience to do Your will and experience the frowns of others, may I know You in such a way that I could sense Your smile upon me." Other people's frowns, anger, and opinions are very visible to us. If we choose to, we may let their views influence us to do the wrong thing or to do something right for the wrong reason. Losing sight of God is often easy when we let displeased human faces block God from our sight.

Trusting God and seeking His face is the best way to respond to difficult situations that become clouded by human reactions and emotions. God is the first person we must please, not our co-workers, friends, or even family. And we do this by seeking His will for us.

Symptom #4: Deserting God when Our Expectations Are Not Met

My senior year in college, I discipled a fellow college student whose mother was very sick. He was earnestly praying for the healing of his mother, just as you and I would do. In this case, the Lord took his mother home to heaven. From that moment on, his heart was cool to the Lord. His idea of God's goodness was wrapped up in God doing a certain thing and coming through in a certain way. All of us are prone to do this, but God wants us to let Him be God and follow Him in obedience, even when we do not immediately agree with or understand His providential dealing in our life.

A student in one of my classes came up to me and said, "I'm relating to a friend of mine who has a lot of intellectual questions about the Christian faith." She began to list a number of questions with the hope that I could say something that might aid her friend.

I happened to ask the right question as I responded, "Has your friend gone through a real disappointment in her life?"

She said, "Well, as a matter of fact her boyfriend broke up with her."

I told the young woman that her friend's real issue was dealing with the breakup, not proving or disproving the Christian faith. Beneath her intellectual questions was deep emotional pain. Her questions were designed to consciously or unconsciously give her a rationale for deserting the God who she thought had let her down when her relationship with her boyfriend had gone bad.

Can we look at life's disappointments in another way? Is God big enough to work good out of your pain and disappointment? I learned a wonderful definition of disappointment many years ago in 1 Peter 4:1–2. "Therefore, since Christ has suffered in the flesh, arm yourselves also with the same purpose, because he who has suffered in the flesh has ceased from sin, so as to live the rest of the time in the flesh no longer for the lusts of men, but for the will of God." If we accept that God loves us and desires the best for us ultimately, then God cannot truly disappoint us. Our disappointments come only from seeking satisfaction from the world first, rather than God's providence. Disappointment is God's way of dimming the glamour of the world and deepening our ability to enjoy Him. It can also even deepen our determination to seek His will if we respond correctly.

Are you willing to tell God about your fear of seeking His will? Has a past disappointment in your life made it hard to open yourself up to God? Are you willing to let God show you that He can bring eternal good out of this pain?

I remember a person who had been abused. This individual had gone through deep pain. However, God had spoken to his heart as he exclaimed, "When I see Jesus hanging on a cross for my sin, I see a totally innocent victim being abused. Perhaps I can identify with Him in a way that you cannot." His pain had been used by God to give him a deeper love for Christ. We too must prayerfully search for the meaning behind our disappointments, while accepting that God loves us and wants to bring us closer to Him.

Symptom #5: Trusting Ourselves More than God

The more something means to us, the harder it is to trust God with it. It may be your future, your child, your spouse or potential mate, or your job. Whatever it is, you may be tempted to control your circumstances and to scheme to get your way.

The man in Scripture most known for his faith is Abraham, who took a courageous step of faith in obedience to God's will (Acts 7:2–5). He was given a number of promises that included the promise that his descendants would form a great nation and that from his descendants the whole world would be blessed (Genesis 12:2–3). God made it clear to him that this would begin with a child who would be born to him in his old age (Genesis 15:4–5). Abraham believed God, but after waiting on God for about sixteen years, his wife Sarah came up with a plan to help God fulfill His promises, by allowing Abraham to father a child with Sarah's maid. Abraham agreed with the scheme (Genesis 16:2–4). Other lapses in Abraham's faith can be seen in Genesis 12 and Genesis 20.

After Isaac was finally born, God brought Abraham to the place of being able to trust God with him. James said in James 2:22 that his "faith was perfected." *Perfect* has the idea of "complete" and "reaching a goal." God presented Abraham with the ultimate test of faith when He instructed Abraham to sacrifice his young son to Him in order to fulfill His promises. When God was satisfied with Abraham's commitment to Him, rather than trusting in his own plans, God spared Isaac and blessed Abraham. God's goal was to bring Abraham to the point that he could completely surrender Isaac into His arms and trust Him with his precious son. Genesis 22 tells this thrilling story, and Hebrews 11:17–19 provides the divine commentary.

What is your "Isaac"? What is so precious to you that it is a great struggle to trust God with it? God's will is to perfect your faith in this matter. He wants to bring you to the point of being able to surrender your "Isaac" to His control. God is honored and pleased with such faith (Hebrews 11:6).

Symptom #6: Failing to Realize the Truth of God's Gifts

"Every good thing given and every perfect gift is from above, coming down from the Father of lights, with whom there is no variation or shifting shadow" (James 1:17).

God is the ultimate source of all blessing. The blessing of guidance is a gift of the Good Shepherd. The gift is only a small reflection of the infinite goodness of the Giver. For years I have kept a diary of each day's activities. I don't spend a lot of time on it, but I do attempt to look at each day in light of James 1:17. I jot down in shorthand form the blessings of each day. There are many blessings that I am not aware of due to my spiritual dullness. However, in spite of this, I see the kindness of God to me though I deserve His wrath.

It's easy to overlook many gifts from God or to attribute them to other sources. The promotion we received at work due to our administrative excellence, for example. Didn't God give us the gift of administration in the first place? Didn't He place us in the right job according to His will? Didn't He grant us the opportunities to excel at work and thus be recognized? As soon as our efforts stop pleasing Him, we can expect the source of goodness in our lives to dry up as well, until we are back in tune with Him. We may still get promoted and get raises, but how satisfied will we be if we aren't living for Him?

Would you consider reviewing your days in light of James 1:17? Remember that each of us has earned God's just condemnation, but in Christ He offers to us His gracious salvation. Everything we receive in life other than His judgment is due to His sovereign grace (Romans 8:32).

Of course this is only a selected list of some of Satan's distorted concepts of God. What others would you add to this list? Satan works tirelessly to bring us down to his own level of failure. He once enjoyed God's grace in abundance, but he threw it away to try to bring himself on par with the Creator of the universe. He's a sore loser. The old expression, "Misery loves company," might have come into being with Satan in mind. Of course, our own fallenness and the fallen world around us also hinder us in our daily struggle to know and honor God.

Ask the Lord for His help. This is a prayer that might help you as you face the daily grind of life, comforted in the fact that you don't have to face it alone: "Heavenly Father, thank You that You have graciously commanded us to honor You alone as our God. Uproot all the thoughts of You in my mind that are not in harmony with Your truth. Teach me to recognize them, reject them, and replace them with the truth of Your Person."

INDICATORS OF FOLLOWING SATAN'S STRATEGY

Detecting whether we are following Satan's strategy may not be as easy as it may at first seem. It is often difficult to examine ourselves in any light, because of our natural built-in biases and perceptions. We may have to rely on other godly people to see these weaknesses in us in order to act upon them. We may sense that something is not right in our walk with God. Most commonly, it comes from a lack of inner satisfaction that we are doing what we are supposed to do, what God wants us to do. The following two indicators are clear evidence of following Satan's strategy for living.

Indicator #1: Pride

Elevating our own stature and image is one of the greatest challenges to pursuing a God-honoring life. Pride has been with man since the beginning. We can see it many times in the Bible, on an individual level, such as King Saul in his later years, or on a collective level, such as the builders of the Tower of Babel. In each case, people sought to affirm their own greatness, to inflate their egos and impress others. Our culture today thrives on pride, proclaiming routinely, "Look what I did," or "Look what we can do." The essence of pride is living independent of God's authority. This was the sin of the devil (1 Timothy 3:6).

SCRIPTURES ON PRIDE

"There are six things which the Lord hates, yes, seven which are an abomination to Him: haughty eyes . . ." (Proverbs 6:16–17a)

"When pride comes, then comes dishonor, but with the humble is wisdom." (Proverbs 11:2)

"The Lord will tear down the house of the proud, but He will establish the boundary of the widow." (Proverbs 15:25)

"Everyone who is proud in heart is an abomination to the Lord; assuredly, he will not be unpunished." (Proverbs 16:5)

"Pride goes before destruction, and a haughty spirit before stumbling." (Proverbs 16:18)

"Haughty eyes and a proud heart, the lamp of the wicked, is sin." (Proverbs 21:4)

"A man's pride will bring him low, but a humble spirit will obtain honor." (Proverbs 29:23)

"But He gives a greater grace. Therefore it says, 'God is opposed to the proud, but gives grace to the humble.'" (James 4:6)

One evidence of pride is a lack of gratitude to God and others. Everything that anyone has ever been able to accomplish is ultimately due to God and usually also some other person. A man who visited Thomas Edison's home in Florida reported that he was fascinated by a stone-lined path in his garden called a "walk of friendship." It was so named because a different close friend gave each stone to Edison. He walked daily in a pathway provided by his friends, who inspired and encouraged him in his work. Every road that has led to the accomplishments in our lives is also due to the contributions of God and others. Humility is seeing God as the source of everything (James 1:17). "A man can receive nothing unless it has been given him from heaven" (John 3:27). A humble person is able to express gratitude to God and to the ones He has used in our lives.

Another evidence is the unwillingness to admit, "I am wrong." Such an admission brings great freedom to the soul as we respond to the conviction of God's Spirit. A humble person is willing to accept the loving rebuke of God and others and to respond appropriately.

Ask God to show you any point of pride in your life that reflects a resistance to His will. God's Spirit seeks to control His people and to produce in us a heart of gratitude, worship, and submission to others (Ephesians 5:18–21). Is there any pursuit in your life that has not been initiated by the Lord? Is there any task that you are doing independently of God? Is there any relationship in which God is not the center? As you respond to God's Spirit in honesty and in repentance, you will be led to the experience of His will.

Indicator #2: Idolatry

Idolatry is always a traveling companion with pride. When we are not in proper fellowship with God, we seek idols to put on His throne. Far from being limited to statues of golden calves or human-shaped figures with animal heads, idols come in many forms, often intangible. Money, career, possessions, habits—all of these can be idols of worship in our lives, displacing our rightfully placed worship to the Lord. Where there is pride, there will be idolatry. Idolatry is a result of separating oneself from God, according to Ezekiel 14:7.

We were created dependent creatures. God designed us to look to Him. If you were perfect in every way, even in your motivations, the greatest gift you could give to someone would be to allow that person to look to you and enjoy you for who you are. This is the heart of our loving Creator. When our pride leads us to live independently of Him, it is inevitable that we look to someone else to meet the God-given need of our heart.

Idolatry is what we look to in order to meet the basic thirsts of our heart. As dependent creatures, we are not self-sufficient, for God created each person with certain basic needs. There have been a number of ways to describe or categorize these needs. For example, every person has a need to feel important and to be secure. You have needs in your heart from which you cannot escape. God designed you in order to look to Him to meet these needs and build a love relationship.

Idols fall into four categories—people, positions, practices, and possessions. You should keep in mind that idols will partly work in the temporal realm. One can find temporary security in a person and a sense of significance in a relationship. One can even establish an identity from his or her job, and this can subtly become an idol. This may be true no matter what the job, even if it is vocational ministry. I remember a friend saying to a minister, "Do you preach because you love the Lord Jesus or because you love to preach?"

There is nothing inherently wrong with most practices or possessions, but they need to be put into perspective. An automobile can be a valuable aid in doing God's work, and it can also become an idol. The same could be said of a house, a computer, or any other possession. Even practices can become idolized in our lives. Watching television, for example (maybe Monday night football for some men), can become a dangerous idol, taking the time that needs to be spent with family or fellowship or worship. I remember the testimony of a very honest person who said, "My wife is an incredible cook. I live to eat!"

Even one's spouse, one's children, or one's friends can become an idol. The obvious truth is that we can make an idol of things that are not inherently evil. One's work, possessions, and family are obvious gifts of God. However, when we expect them to do for us what only God can do, we will be led to sorrow and disappointment. "The sorrows of those who have bartered for another god will be multiplied" (Psalm 16:4). Only

God can give the promise, "Whoever believes in [Me] will not be disappointed" (Romans 10:11).

Ask God to uncover the idols of your life. What do you look to in order to meet the desires and thirsts of your heart? Ask Him to meet those deepest longings that drive you toward some idol. Only His Spirit can enable you to keep the people, positions, possessions, and practices in your life in proper perspective.

THE FRUIT OF SATAN'S STRATEGY

What is the result of following Satan's strategy? We have stated that pride and idolatry are two indicators that we are following Satan's plan. What do they always result in? Futility. A pursuit of God's will must recognize that anything done independent of God is futile and produces only vanity. Anytime we depart from God we are pursuing futility, according to 1 Samuel 12:20–21. Look it up! Your pursuit of God's will must first of all be a pursuit of God Himself. "Unless the Lord builds the house, they labor in vain who build it; Unless the Lord guards the city, the watchman keeps awake in vain" (Psalm 127:1). If God is not in it, it is futility. The key is not to work harder. "It is vain for you to rise up early, to retire late, to eat the bread of painful labors; for He gives to His beloved even in his sleep" (Psalm 127:2).

Jesus stated the same truth when He said to His disciples, "I am the vine, you are the branches; he who abides in Me and I in him, he bears much fruit, for apart from Me you can do nothing" (John 15:5). Whether it is God's plan for you to be a doctor, a lawyer, a farmer, a businessman, a housewife, single or married, it is clearly His plan for you to learn to live in harmony with Him.

A life apart from God will result in staleness and emptiness. There may be temporary "highs" from pursuing worldly delights, but in the end, you will see them for the hollow rewards they are, devoid of the love, meaning, and permanence that characterize God's gifts. Someone related to me a conversation between two friends in which one asked the question, "What do you want from life?" When there was no response the inquirer said, "You want more." The friend agreed wholeheartedly. When the first friend asked him if he would ever get enough, he replied, "No, I guess I never will." In fact a reporter once asked the billionaire John D. Rockefeller how much money it would take to make him happy. He replied, "Just a little bit more." We too will never get enough from the world, for the world doesn't have the right substance to fill us—only God does.

I have read that the people in North Africa capture a monkey by making a hole in a gourd that is the size of the monkey's hand. Then they fill the gourd with nuts and tie it to a tree. As the monkey reaches into the gourd for the nuts he discovers that he cannot pull his hand out of the gourd. You can easily see that all he has to do is to let go of the nuts. However, he ends up being captured because of his greed.

Are you willing to release your hold on anything that is causing you to sin? Are you willing to come to grip with the radical truth of John 15:5, "I am the vine, you are the branches; he who abides in Me and I in him, he bears much fruit, for apart from Me you can do nothing"?

I remember a difficult time in my own life during one Christmas holiday. After much struggle to conduct the Christian life in my own strength and facing spiritual discouragement resulting from my failure, I clearly felt God's rebuke. I had been trying to bear fruit on my own. My clearest memory of this experience is coming to the realization that I did not really believe John 15:5. It is indeed a radical truth! If we do accept it, it is only logical to have as our first priority learning to abide in Him. God does not command us to do something that He will not also make a reality in our lives as we look to Him. Life with Christ is an endless hope; life without Him is a hopeless end.

After graduating from high school, I joined the Air Force Reserves. I spent six months on active duty and then began my studies at Auburn University where I decided to major in business. I joined my brother's social fraternity, made excellent grades, and received various honors. Outwardly, my life was going great, but inwardly, it was full of the fears of rejection and failure.

I walked into a fraternity brother's room, and he began telling me about the ministry of the Holy Spirit. Buster was one of the most unusual persons I had ever met. I had never met an individual who took such a stand for Christ in an environment where it was not at all popular to do so. He had pledged our social fraternity for the expressed purpose of leading men to Christ. Listening that day as he talked with me, I began processing the truths I heard but did not respond in any way. However, as my roommate was moving out and so was his, I asked Buster if I could move in with him. We roomed together for one year. God used that year with Robert "Buster" Holmes to draw me into a surrender of my life to the Lord. I thought that I had been genuinely converted six years earlier and had sought to read the Bible each day. However, I was not living in a way that allowed the Lord to influence the ambitions and goals of my life. Then I went home one weekend from college, knelt in the privacy of my own room, and told the Lord that I wanted to present my life to Him and attempt to live like Buster.

This decision put my life on the pathway of consciously pursuing God's will. I began to be confronted with my wrong ideas of God and my life of pride and idolatry. Wherever the Lord finds you, let me assure you that when you surrender your life to Him, He will unveil His will for your life.

NOTE: To reflect on what we have explored so far, go to the personal journal on page 190.

Developing a Relationship with God

◆

Chapter Three

Trusting and
Delighting
in God

H elen Carruthers is in a quandary. She has worked hard and sacrificed much to become the leading salesperson at MacGraw Electronics, a midsized computer and electronic components manufacturer. Despite the constant pressures of making budget, she had managed to do that and rear a family and manage a household, no mean feat for a forty-year-old mother of two. She had also managed to remain a strong and committed believer, attending church and a ladies' Bible study regularly.

Up until now, though, the key to her success had been that she was able to remain local, traveling in and around the St. Paul–Minneapolis area where she worked and lived. She had arranged a work schedule that enabled her to get her two middle schoolers off to school in the morning and be home shortly after they got off the bus in the afternoon. She was thus able to keep a relatively stable routine and devote time to her family.

Last week, her boss, impressed by her success, offered her a big promotion: regional sales manager. It was a job normally reserved for more senior sales staff. It involved the supervision of a dozen sales people in seven states. It was a great opportunity for her. The catch: She would have to travel—a lot.

Helen senses that God is involved in this job development, but she doesn't know what God's will is. Should she choose the job and increase her income but see less of her family? Or should she turn down the job offer, retaining her stable family life but possibly jeopardizing her future with the company? She has to make a decision soon. She wants to trust God, but He might take too long to help her decide. Or He might not understand her career ambitions. Or He might never give her another opportunity if she passes this one by. Like many others, she feels alone.

In his book *The Knowledge of the Holy,* A. W. Tozer stated, "What comes to our minds when we think about God is the most important thing about us."[1] He went on to say, "Were we able to extract from any man a complete answer to the question, 'What comes into your mind when you think about God?' we might predict with certainty the spiritual future of that man."[2]

A number of years ago, our college decided to put together a new required freshman course entitled Christian Life and Ethics. I was one of the professors who was asked to teach this course. Having seen fruit in people's lives that had come from focusing on God's character, I sensed that it would be helpful to include a brief section on the attributes of God. But in developing the course, I saw that emphasizing God's character should be the foundation for the entire course. I asked myself the following questions as I worked on the curriculum:

1. How could I talk about trusting God if I did not train the student in knowing God? (cf. Psalm 9:10)
2. How could I talk about presenting one's life to the Lord if I did not talk about the merciful heavenly Father to whom we present our lives? (Romans 12:1–2)
3. How could I talk about loving God if I did not talk first about His love for us? (1 John 4:19)
4. How could I talk about fearing God if I did not talk about knowing God, since the knowledge of God's character is what produces a fear of God? (Proverbs 2:5)

It became obvious to me that no class about living the successful Christian life could be taught without knowing and accepting God's character. Although teaching this at first seemed a diversion from learning how to confront the nitty-gritty, daily applications of Christian ethics, the students had (and continue to have) a greater appreciation for understanding and living the Christian lifestyle.

God Himself confirms the importance of knowing His character in 2 Corinthians 3:18: "But we all, with unveiled face, beholding as in a mirror the glory of the Lord, are being transformed into the same image from glory to glory, just as from the Lord, the Spirit." A focus on God's glorious character is the means that the Lord uses to transform a life! Only the transforming of our thoughts about God will produce genuine and lasting changes in our lives, and the primary aspect of God's will is to conform us to the image of Christ (Romans 8:29). Earl Radmacher, formerly president of Western Seminary, wrote, "Right living begins with right thinking. And right thinking begins with right thinking about God."[3]

Let's look at a life that unquestionably accomplished the will of God. The apostle Paul said at the end of his life, "I have fought the good fight, I have finished the course, I have kept the faith" (2 Timothy 4:7). No doubt accomplishing God's will was the absolute priority of his life, for he said, "I do not consider my life of any account as dear to myself, so that I may finish my course" (Acts 20:24).

What was the focus of this "successful" man in God's eyes? He stated it in the words "that I may know Him" (Philippians 3:10). God's will is to build in you and me a determination to do the will of God. This is one aspect of Christlikeness (John 4:34). It is also His will that this be carried out in communion with Him every step of the way (John 5:19; 15:5).

As you pursue God's will you may need to adjust

the focus of your pursuit. It is better to pursue a life of understanding and knowing God as you pursue God's will. The acid test for gauging God's pleasure in us in spelled out clearly in Jeremiah 9:23–24.

> *Thus says the Lord, "Let not a wise man boast of his wisdom, and let not the mighty man boast of his might, let not a rich man boast of his riches; but let him who boasts boast of this, that he understands and knows Me, that I am the Lord who exercises lovingkindness, justice, and righteousness on earth; for I delight in these things," declares the Lord.*

What does it mean to understand and know God? Perhaps it will help us to see the difference between understanding and knowing. To understand God is to comprehend truths about God. I can comprehend that He is trustworthy, but I do not *know* it until I trust Him with the concern of my heart at this moment. He desires us to learn truths about Him, but also to interact with these truths in our experience. He can disclose to us that He is lovable and delightful, but I do not begin to know that in my experience until I begin to learn what it means to love Him and delight in Him.

This focus should not be misunderstood so that we conclude that God can be understood and experienced in a way that is unrelated to life—God has a work for each of us to do (Ephesians 2:10). But as we do this work, our focus is to be on Him. If you are a husband, you have the responsibility of providing for your family. However, God wants your focus to be getting to know God as your "Jehovah Jireh," which means "The Lord who Provides." My wife told me, "As I grew up I knew God as Jehovah Jireh through my daddy, but since I've been married to you I feel like I have a more direct link." This is no credit to me but only to a merciful God who has met her in her need.

This focus does not mean that God does not want you also to be productive in your life. The apostle Paul was an incredibly productive person with a fruitful ministry, but his focus was always to know Christ (Philippians 3:10). The Lord Jesus did the Father's will perfectly because His continual focus was on the Father (John 17:4).

Have you ever sought to communicate God's Word and become disillusioned because people did not seem to be interested? Have you ever felt like giving up? Have you ever felt that your work as a housewife was not being appreciated in the way your heart needs to be appreciated? God wants you to continue in the work that He has given you to do but to focus on getting to know Him better. Let all your needs and frustrations lead you to Him, for He is the focus that will give meaning to the picture that God is painting through your life.

UNDERSTANDING AND KNOWING
A GOD WHO IS TRUSTWORTHY

For us to devote our life's work and purpose to God, we must be convinced that our efforts will be rewarded. Our own nature causes us to look questioningly on any work that has no rewards or benefits. How long would you remain behind your window at the post office, selling stamps and weighing packages, if you never got paid?

Here are three foundational principles that will help you to know and accept that God is worthy of your trust and love.

1. *God has unlimited resources.* "All things are possible with God," according to Mark 10:27. Your needs are no strain on God. Your problems are not beyond His power to love. *The maker of Creation transcends all physical laws and limitations.* But what is God's attitude toward you? This brings us to the second principle.

2. *God delights in His children.* I remember the first time this truth hit me. I was driving my car on a trip to L.A. (Lower Alabama). That morning I was reading Psalm 18. I do not think that I have ever gotten over the impact of verse 19. "He [God] rescued me, because He delighted in me." God *delights* in me who has given Him so many reasons not to—yet He does. False humility can make a person afraid to agree with this great truth. I remember a sweet, precious student who thought it was an act of pride to say that God loved her. She evidently thought that this meant that she was deserving of His love, as

opposed to humbling herself before God and enjoying the blessing of His gracious love.

3. *God desires to be trusted.* If a child went around the house biting his fingernails in constant anxiety over whether his parents would feed him, this would bring great dishonor to them. God wants His children to live with confidence even when they feel very needy. The godly person will not be impressed at all with his godliness. He will be impressed with his total need of God. But in our neediness we can still be secure. Even though we do not know how something is going to work out, we can look to God and trust Him and be willing to do whatever He wants us to do. Faith brings great pleasure to the heart of God (Hebrews 11:6).

People can misunderstand these foundational principles as they get to know a God who is trustworthy. One might reason, "Since You have unlimited resources and You delight in me, then give me three new Cadillacs!" God loves us so much that He has not placed on us the burden of living under the lordship of our own desires. In other words, it is not totally up to us to figure out what is best for us. I like this definition of God's will: "God's will is exactly what you could desire if you knew all the facts." Since only God knows all the facts, we have to admit that we might be deceived in our thinking about what we desire. The position we are to take in faith is, "What do You want me to trust You for, Lord?" Commit your desires to Him and trust Him with the dark times when it seems God is not being attentive to you.

The apostle Paul asked God to remove his "thorn in the flesh." Whatever it was, it was something very unpleasant, and he strongly wanted it to be removed. God did not give Paul his request, but instead He gave him an even greater desire. Paul's longing was to be as useful a Christian as possible. God knew this and gave him a greater enablement to serve others (2 Corinthians 12:7–10). God did not answer the request of his lips, but He did answer the deepest desire of his heart.

Faith is ceasing to trust in yourself and placing all of your confidence in God. He is the only worthy object of your faith. At the conclusion of my doctoral program, I was getting ready for a series of written exams. Returning early to school in order to prepare, I realized I was not ready, but I thought, *Give me a little time and I'll be ready.* The next day I woke up very sick and was totally incapacitated for a few days. The day I was well enough to get up, I read Psalm 30:6–7, "But as for me, I said in my prosperity, 'I will never be moved.' O Lord, by Your favor You have made my mountain to stand strong; You hid Your face, I was dismayed." I felt rebuked for my attitude in thinking that all I needed was a little time and I could do it. My faith was in my ability and not in God who controls my health and even my very life breath.

How can you tell that you are living by faith? We'd like to be able to look in the mirror in the morning and somehow see the light of God upon our brow, but that isn't the way it works. Or it would be good to get a telegram placed under our pillow at night that said, "Well done, good and faithful servant. Signed, God." But that doesn't happen either. So how can we judge for ourselves that we are being faithful to all that the Father wants for us? Here are three outward expressions of faith we should look for.

1. *Our speech.* Jesus stated, "For his mouth speaks from that which fills his heart" (Luke 6:45). Our speech, especially our unplanned speech, reveals the faith or unbelief of our hearts. God desires us not to be phony in our speech, for He desires "truth in the innermost being" (Psalm 51:6). He encourages us to pour out our hearts before Him as the Psalms demonstrate. But that does not mean demanding that God meet our every expectation or else explain Himself. Our grumbling can reflect such attitudes as "God, You are not adequate" or "God, You are not really in control" or "God, You are not good." An example of faith is coming to Jesus with our helplessness.

2. *Obedience.* Every step of genuine obedience is a step of faith. Warren Wiersbe said, "Faith is obeying God in spite of feelings, circumstances, or consequences." Romans 1:5 speaks of the obedience of faith when it says, "Through whom we have received grace and apostleship to bring about the obedience of faith among all

the Gentiles for His name's sake." Our initial step of faith is obeying God's command to place our complete confidence in the Lord Jesus for our salvation. This is the beginning of a relationship that is to be characterized by a faith that obeys God's Word.

3. *Facing our fears and anxieties.* Jesus spoke to His disciples in a very perplexed moment in their lives and said, "Do not let your heart be troubled; believe in God, believe also in Me" (John 14:1). George Mueller said that the beginning of anxiety is the end of faith, and the beginning of faith is the end of anxiety. As long as we live in this unredeemed world we will be tempted by fear and anxiety, and the first step in dealing with them is to admit that we are fearful and anxious. Worry is unbelief in disguise. The greatest fears are probably the fear of failure and the fear of rejection. Pride will seek to cover our problem and look to some "fix" (idol) to deal with it, but God invites us to seek Him rather than be consumed by fear. Psalm 34:4 says, "I sought the Lord, and He answered me, and delivered me from all my fears." God commands the believer to "be anxious for nothing," and He graciously instructs the believer how to trust Him with anxiety.

Philippians 4:6–7 tells us that prayer + supplication + thanksgiving = God's peace. *Every time we are tempted to be anxious, God prompts us to pray or talk with Him.* You may need to ask Him to show you what is the root of your anxiety. To supplicate God is to ask Him specifically for what you would like Him to do about your concern. Sometimes I've found it helpful to write down my supplication and document it with Scripture that is relevant to my issue. Be alert to times when God desires to provide a friend to pray with you, for He is seeking not only to meet your need but also to deepen the relationships of your life.

If your prayers are limited to supplication, you will tend to get wrapped up in your problem. Thanksgiving lifts our hearts to God. We can thank Him that He has invited us to pray and He hears our prayer. We can also thank Him that He is in control and has a deep concern for us. The result is the experience of the peace of God, which Jesus called "rest for your souls" (Matthew 11:29).

An important aspect of this process of faith is learning to live one day at a time and not to be anxious about tomorrow—even being anxious about finding God's will. Worry is nothing more than borrowed trouble. As some unknown author wrote, "Worry does not relieve tomorrow of its stress, it merely empties today of its strength."

UNDERSTANDING AND KNOWING A GOD WHO IS DELIGHTFUL

One of the most attractive promises in the Bible is the promise that "He will give you the desires of your heart" (Psalm 37:4). The promise is conditioned upon the preceding command, "Delight yourself in the Lord." One of the great roadblocks in the pursuit of God's will is *confusing which is your part and which is God's part.* The world trains us to delight in the desires of our hearts and seek to fulfill them *ourselves.* God's Word tells us that seeking self-satisfaction will cause us disappointment and bring us into conflict with those who cannot satisfy our needs (James 4:1–2). God's way is for us to seek the things that will satisfy Him, and His blessing of inner joy and fulfillment will be His gift to us.

In understanding that God is delightful, a good place to start is with the truth that God is a person, because we understand what it means to delight in another person. Let's look at some potential applications we can use.

1. *Delighting in His presence.* When we delight in a person, we enjoy being with that person. Delighting in God involves cultivating a continuous enjoyment in His presence. We will explore this more in another chapter.

2. *Delighting in His conversation.* Delighting in a person involves delighting in the joy of both talking to that individual and listening to him. When the Scripture describes a godly person, it speaks of his delight in God's Word and of his continual meditation upon it (Psalm 1:2).

3. *Delighting in His accomplishments.* "Great are the works of the Lord; they are studied by all who

delight in them" (Psalm 111:2). This involves not only His great works of creation and salvation, but also His continual works that He desires to do each day in and through us. Our attitude of each day is to be that which Paul stated, "The life which I now live in the flesh I live by faith in the Son of God, who loved me and gave Himself up for me" (Galatians 2:20). Each day is to be a day of allowing God to work out His desires in and through us in the midst of the routines of life. Keeping a diary of what God does and how He provides for us can aid in delighting in His accomplishments.

4. *Delighting in His desires.* When you delight in someone, you delight in what delights him or her. Second Corinthians 5:9 states Paul's ambition with the words "to be pleasing to Him." Delighting in God involves delighting in bringing pleasure to God! Although a person who has trusted Jesus cannot be separated from God's love (Romans 8:38–39), it is an appropriate goal to learn to please the Lord (Ephesians 5:10). A believer in Christ does not need to strive to be accepted by God, but rather to find delight in pleasing God. To experience the joy at bringing pleasure to God is to be the greatest priority of a believer's life (Galatians 1:10), and Hebrews 11:6 tells us that the key to this is faith.

5. *Delighting in His delight in us.* We loved because God first loved us (1 John 4:19). Our delight in

God is only a response to His delight in us (Psalm 18:19). Can you imagine someone who knew everything about you—all you have ever thought, said, and done—finding delight in you? I got an idea from a godly friend and I'll pass it along to you. Based on the Father's perfect love for His Son and His perfect love for us in Christ (John 17:26), he begins his letter to his daughter with this phrase, "This is my beloved daughter in whom I am well-pleased." It is God's will for you to accept this truth for yourself and then pass it on to your loved ones. The pathway of trusting God and delighting in Him will lead you to the experience of His will.

Trusting and delighting in God is not just a mental exercise that makes us feel better. It can and should be a vibrant part of our spiritual lives. If we trust in the Gospel and its explanation for human purpose and destiny, then we must trust what it says about God to be true. We must sense God as a real and living Being, not in an abstract plane of existence, but here with us now, watching us, advising us, safeguarding us, and loving us.

When we trust in God, we will also find it possible to delight in Him, for the creation around us is His gift and reflects His glory. Goodness, order, reason, peace, compassion, and fulfillment find their ultimate origin in Him. The knowledge and understanding that He devoted His time and energy to craft us, along with all we are, should cause us to delight in Him, for we are shadowy images of Him. All the goodness that we enjoy is due to Him. The next time you savor that delicious piece of fruit or homemade bread, keep in mind who allowed you to experience that sensation and gave you the taste buds to enjoy it. The next time you experience the love of a brother or sister, remember the source of all true love. He is the only worthy object of our complete trust and delight.

NOTES

1. A. W. Tozer, *The Knowledge of the Holy* (San Francisco: Harper, 1978), 9.
2. Ibid.
3. Earl Radmacher, *You & Your Thoughts* (Wheaton, Ill.: Tyndale, 1977), 41.

◆

Chapter Four

Understanding God's Will for All of His Children

T hree centuries before Christ was born, and shortly after the death of Alexander the Great, many
educated Greeks held to a new philosophy called sto-
icism. Stoics, followers of this philosophy, held to the
belief that people could know the will of the gods by
understanding and conforming to the world around
them.

If, for example, you were walking in the country
when it started to rain, it was the gods' will that you
get wet, especially if you hadn't brought an umbrella
or any rain gear with you. Worrying about staying dry
or getting under cover was irrelevant, if circumstances
had placed you in a position where these options were
not available.

This philosophy was reassuring to many Greeks who were frustrated by ineffectual attempts to know the will of the gods through divination, animal sacrifices, or prayers from mediums and priests. If one led a simple, austere life, unfettered by worries about the future or anxious prayers to a remote god or gods, one could expect to receive a general revelation of the gods' will for him or her.

If you were born poor, your father was a stonemason, and you were physically unattractive, it would be only natural to accept that you too would be poor, be a stonemason, and, at best, marry a poor, plain-looking woman. Unless the gods intervened in some way, your life's destiny was largely known already. Acceptance of this would make you happy. What will be, will be.

What the stoics thought about the meaning of life was partially correct, insofar as it applied to the world. Each of us is born into certain circumstances, which, in our own efforts, we are unlikely to alter much. If you are tall and agile, you will have a decided advantage over others when playing basketball.

What the stoics missed out on was the very nature of the real and living God, the Creator of the universe. Their "gods" were a distant, changeable presence, making themselves known when the occasion suited. Our God is a real and personal Being, who made us in His likeness and with a plan for each of us to fulfill His will while on earth. Far from being distant, God speaks to us daily and intimately through His Word.

Rather than relying on a "what will be, will be" sort

of philosophy, we can seek His will by knowing God, seeking to conform to His character, and keeping open a continual line of communication to Him with our prayers. To be sure, God gave us certain physical qualities and gifts that He intends for us to use, but He also seeks to mold and use us to fulfill His will and to glorify Him in view of creation. And to do this, we must surrender our wills to Him and know Him as our loving Father and Savior.

At the base of the matter of knowing God's will is the question, "How do I sense that I am fulfilling His will?" To get a clearer understanding of this question of knowing God's will for His children, let us look at four ways in which we can sense God's confirmation. When we can see and sense satisfaction in these areas, our sense of having fulfilled God's will becomes more apparent.

GOD'S WILL THAT YOU
THINK RIGHTLY ABOUT YOURSELF

If I were to ask you, "What affects your view of yourself more than anything else?" how would you respond? The greatest factor in determining your own self-assessment is probably your perception of what the most important person in your life thinks about you. The more important a person is to you, the more you weigh your perception of what he or she thinks about you.

I took a trip one May to England to visit a friend

who was studying at Manchester University. When I was jogging along a street in town, two pedestrians stopped to look at me. After a brief moment, they both broke out into loud laughter. Evidently, they found my jogging suit, or my jog, quite humorous. I broke out in a laugh also. I had never seen these people before and would probably never see them again. Their perception of me had very little effect on my view of myself. However, if I went to the breakfast table at home one morning and my wife and sons all pointed at me and started to laugh, I would be more self-conscious.

It is God's will for you to establish Him as the most important input into your life. A right view of yourself is a product of listening to Him and rejecting the input in your life that is not in harmony with His perspective. If you have sensed your complete need of God's forgiveness and placed your trust in Jesus, you can know just how valuable you are to Him. Throughout the Bible, God tells His people that they are precious to Him. Look at these summary points of several Scripture passages that reflect God's thinking about His children.

1. "I accept you" (Romans 15:7).
2. "You are a precious person to me, and I am continually thinking about you" (Psalm 139:17–18).
3. "I'm continually devoted to you and will provide all that you need to fulfill My purpose for you" (Romans 8:31–32, 38–39).

4. "I've adopted you into My family and will take care of you, lead you, discipline you, and develop you as your Father" (Galatians 4:5–6).
5. "I'll live in you, and you'll never have to be alone as I had to be when I died on the cross for you" (Galatians 2:20; Hebrews 13:5b).
6. "I have a wonderful future for you, that you will know joy and satisfaction for all eternity" (Romans 8:18).
7. "I have a unique plan of good works for you to accomplish" (Ephesians 2:10).
8. "My plan is unique for you because no one else has your exact physical features, upbringing, talents, and abilities, and even your unique weaknesses" (Psalm 139:13–16).
9. "I'll continue to work in you because My glory is at stake" (Philippians 2:13; Psalm 23:3).
10. "I'll make you into a most attractive person in My eyes and allow you to fulfill My plan as you present your life to Me" (Romans 8:29; 12:1–2).

Do you believe these amazing truths? Reread point 8! For which one of your features do you struggle to thank God? Helen Keller, who was deaf and mute, said, "I thank God for my handicaps, for through them, I have found myself, my work, and my God." There should be no doubt after reading these verses that God is serious about His relationship with you. Read Point 9 again. God is committed to His children because His glory is at stake. God's very essence demands that He bolster the relationship of trust and faith with us.

God wants you to have a right view about yourself as a child of God, because that will manifest itself in your relationship with Him and with others. You are not perfect in your Christian experience, but God recognizes this and will work in your life to bring about the fulfillment of His will for you, as you accept His sovereignty in your life. One aspect of understanding His will for you is getting a proper perception of yourself as a child of God.

GOD'S WILL THAT YOU HAVE MEANING AND PURPOSE IN YOUR LIFE

The only way to have real meaning and purpose in one's life is to have a right relationship with the Creator. We have been created by God and for God (Colossians 1:16). A person who has real meaning in life can find purpose in the routine of life. So much of life is lived in a routine. Brushing one's teeth, taking out the garbage, paying the bills, and countless other routine things are a significant part of most of our lives. God tells us, "Whether, then, you eat or drink or whatever you do, do all to the glory of God" (1 Corinthians 10:31). When you have a relationship with God, you have something worth dying for. If you don't have something worth dying for, you will not have anything worth living for—and this will be evident in the routine of your life.

Although most of life is lived in a routine, it is not to be so routine that we lose sight of loving God as the greatest priority in all of life. Any moment in life, no matter how routine, is an opportunity to fellowship with the Lord. Even the mundane elements of life can have rich meaning and purpose as we abide in the Lord. Abiding in the Lord involves trusting, submitting to, and obeying God. Our daily life should be one of continual and complete dependence on the Lord (Galatians 2:20). In the words of the psalmist, we are to commit everything to Him and to trust Him with it. He will show us our part and we can watch Him work (Psalm 37:5). Hudson Taylor stated his experience of learning to abide this way, "I used to ask God to help me. Then I asked if I might help Him. I ended up by asking Him to do His work through me." As we live life in this way, we will be prepared for any special opportunity that God gives us. Billy Graham was once asked what it was like speaking to the royal family of England. He said, "I always speak before the Lord of lords and the Kings of kings. It wasn't that different."

A person who understands the true meaning and purpose of life has been able to overcome the boredom factor in his or her life. One of the most gracious commands God ever gives is to present the totality of our life to Him (Romans 12:1–2). All the various parts of our body can become "instruments of righteousness" (Romans 6:13). God has given each of us certain aptitudes, talents, and abilities. Many "successful" people have distinguished careers and yet are deeply bored with their lives. Why are they bored? Their job only requires a certain percentage of their ability, say 60 percent. The result is a 40 percent boredom factor.

God in His mercy encourages us to present the totality of our lives to Him. He desires that we commit all of ourselves into the hands of our Creator. This is what gives a person real meaning and purpose. You may not even fully understand some of the abilities and gifts that God has given you because they have not yet been fully developed. When we make ourselves available to the Lord, He helps us discover and develop every facet of our lives. You may say, "I'm at a job that doesn't require all of me." You can still place the totality of your life in God's hand, do your job for Him, and stay there until God opens a door to something else. He never wastes what you entrust to Him.

GOD'S WILL FOR YOU
TO EXPERIENCE CONTENTMENT

Bill Gothard defines contentment as "realizing that God has provided everything I need for my present happiness." God desires you to be free from the strain and pull of having to get ahead. He wants you free from being controlled by the desire of status, possessions, and position. He desires you to be able to enjoy His gracious provisions.

I remember Dr. John Walvoord speaking in a chapel service one day and relating how God called him into the ministry. As a young boy he went to hear a pastor who served in a very small church. Walvoord could not even remember his name or anything he said, but what struck him was the way in which this pastor reflected contentment in his seemingly obscure station in life. Walvoord absorbed that simple, sincere contentment of the pastor, and it stirred up in him a desire for the ministry. When this unknown pastor stands before the throne of God, he will be rewarded for his part in making possible the numerous books that Dr. Walvoord would later write and for Dr. Walvoord's able administrative work as pastor, professor, president, and chancellor of Dallas Theological Seminary.

As you seek God's will, remember that God wants to teach you contentment in whatever circumstance you presently find yourself (Philippians 4:11–12). The secret to this contentment is our relationship with Christ, who promises to give us the strength to do all that He has for us (Philippians 4:13). As Paul wrote these words, he was in jail, but he always knew that he was in Christ.

One of the greatest expressions of contentment is found in Psalm 73:25, "Whom have I in heaven but You? And besides You, I desire nothing on earth." All that one needs to be content is Christ and what Christ chooses to provide. A lack of contentment will tempt you to get off track in seeking God's will. Rather, let this lack of contentment draw you to Christ (John 7:37–39). When you long for another person, position, or possession, you are experiencing the same yearning that God has toward you at that moment. He sent His Son to die for you in your rebellious, godless, and helpless state in order to give you every spiritual blessing in Christ (Romans 5:6–8; Ephesians 1:3). Why would you not desire to allow such a loving Person to control your life?

GOD'S WILL FOR YOU TO BE SECURE

Security is the fruit of knowing the sovereign God and developing a relationship with Him. Romans 8:28 is one of the most comforting verses in the Bible. While there are some things we do not know, everyone who loves Christ can know that God is ruling and overruling every event in his life for his eternal good. The "all" things of Romans 8:28 means "all"! Things that are not good in isolation can be overruled to "work together" for our eternal good. God took the cruelest event that has ever happened—the crucifixion of Jesus—and turned it into the greatest blessing that the world has ever known (Acts 2:23).

Security is found in realizing how God defines "good." Good is being conformed to the image of God's Son (Romans 8:29). This includes such things as the ability to experience peace in the midst of great stress (John 14:27), the joy of obeying God (John 15:10–11), and the achievement of genuine success (John 17:4). This is the expression of the secure trust of an unknown author: "I may not understand, Lord, but one day shall see, Thy loving hand was taking pains to fashion me like Thee."

Your very interest in pursuing God's will is a reflection of God's work in conforming you to the image of His Son. In Christ we see a single-minded determination to do the Father's will and His complete submission to and dependence upon the Father. Look at the following Scripture texts that reflect this aspect of Christlikeness.

"My food is to do the will of Him who sent Me and to accomplish His work." (John 4:34)

"I can do nothing on My own initiative. As I hear, I judge; and My judgment is just, because I do not seek My own will, but the will of Him who sent Me." (John 5:30)

"For I have come down from heaven, not to do My own will, but the will of Him who sent Me." (John 6:38)

"He who speaks from himself seeks his own glory; but He who is seeking the glory of the One who sent Him, He is true, and there is no unrighteousness in Him." (John 7:18)

"But I do not seek My glory; there is One who seeks and judges." (John 8:50)

"We must work the works of Him who sent Me as long as it is day; night is coming when no one can work." (John 9:4)

"For I did not speak on My own initiative, but the Father Himself who sent Me has given Me a commandment as to what to say and what to speak. I know that His commandment is eternal life; therefore the things I speak, I speak just as the Father has told Me." (John 12:49–50)

"But so that the world may know that I love the Father, I do exactly as the Father commanded Me. Get up, let us go from here." (John 14:31)

The decision Jesus made in that last passage led to the greatest statement of success that has ever been recorded. "I glorified You on the earth, having accomplished the work which You have given Me to do" (John 17:4).

The apostle Paul encouraged others to imitate him as he imitated Christ (1 Corinthians 11:1). Part of this imitation was his determination to do the Father's will. He said that finishing God's "course" for him and completing the ministry that he had received was more dear to him than his own life! (Acts 20:24). This determination and disciplined dependence upon Christ (Galatians 2:20) enabled him to state at the end of his life—"I have fought the good fight, I have finished the course, I have kept the faith" (2 Timothy 4:7).

The achievement of this type of godly success involved times of preparation. Jesus had thirty "silent" years before the three years of His public ministry. Paul spent time in Arabia in preparation for his public ministry. Moses spent forty years tending sheep prior to his ministry to the nation of Israel. John the Baptist spent time in the wilderness before his public ministry began. The silence of Scripture in regard to what happened during these preparatory years speaks loudly. The tendency for us would be to devise a curriculum and attempt to put everyone through it in order to be prepared. But the preparation for each of us is personal. All of us can trust in Him for the very best preparation and education we need to fulfill His plan for us.

We are uncertain of many things that face us in the future, but we do know that it will involve the need to know God in order to know His will. The following is a prayer that God desires to answer in your life.

"God, I want to know You above all else in life. I need the motivation, encouragement, and the wisdom to know how; but I desire it and want to desire it more. I believe You will overcome all obstacles and accomplish this in my life!

"For Your name's sake and for my eternal benefit, Amen."

NOTE: To reflect on what we have explored so far, go to the personal journal on page 192.

Section Three

◆

Knowing God's Character in Order to Discern His Will

Chapter Five

The Person of God

G od's will was not a topic I enjoyed lecturing on in the past. I remember hearing two godly men referring to the confusion among listeners that often resulted after their speaking on this topic.

One year, I was assigned to teach a course that required me to know and discuss this subject. I greatly struggled to put together a couple of lectures on knowing God's will. Later, I was asked to teach a radio series on this topic that would involve sixty-five brief broadcasts entitled "How to Know God's Will." My first response was to wonder, *How could I speak sixty-five times on this subject?* As I walked to the commuter train from work that day, a thought came to my mind that gave me the courage to accept the offer to do the radio series.

I sensed that much of the confusion in this matter of God's will comes when there is a greater desire to know God's will than to know God Himself. The conviction that the revelation of God's character is the proper framework for experiencing God's will has been growing ever since. Let us take time to examine some of the attributes that God has revealed about His person and how a proper response to them leads us to the experience of learning God's will.

GOD IS A PERSON

Dr. W. A. Criswell, pastor of the First Baptist Church of Dallas for many years, told this story. He said that if Jesus were living today and came to a group of modern theologians and philosophers and asked them, "Who do men say that I am?" He might get this response: "Thou art the ground of being. Thou art the leap of faith into the imperishable unknown. Thou art the existential, unphraseable, unverbalized, unpropositional constantation with the infinitude of inherent subjective experience." Criswell said that Jesus' response would be, "Huh?"

Sometimes we can treat our God very impersonally. The supreme revelation of God was in the person of the Lord Jesus Christ. God is revealed in Scripture as a person, One who speaks, sees, hears, delights, and sorrows. God's will is that we respond to this truth and enter into a personal relationship with Him. One can trust Jesus Christ as his or her Savior and have peace with God (Romans 5:1). Such a relationship enables you to view God not only as the Sovereign of the entire world but also as One who is working in, ruling, and overruling all of your circumstances and activities. It enables you to know God not only as One who loves the world, but who also intimately loves you.

When we lose sight of knowing God as our personal heavenly Father, our Christian lives dwindle to a life of traditions and rituals (Galatians 4:8–11). God has given us the Holy Spirit to lead us into an intimacy that enables us to relate to Him as our "Abba, Father" (Romans 8:14–15). *Abba* is the Greek transliteration of the Aramaic word for father and is kin to the way many of us use "Daddy."

Jesus honored His followers by not only calling them His friends but also by stating the responsibility and privilege of this title (John 15:14–15). The responsibility is to obey Him, and the privilege is to be the recipient of the revelation of God. All that we need to know to do God's will He will show us.

In my first year of graduate study I pleaded with God to show me my future ministry with great clarity. I was impressed with how God had laid the country of China on the heart of Hudson Taylor and how he focused all of his preparation toward that goal. I told God that if He would give me a vision for my future, I also would focus all my preparation toward this goal. When I told this prayer burden to a pastor I was serving, he wisely told me, "Bill, you are the kind of person that if you knew your future with that kind of clarity, you would be tempted to grow discontent in the present." God has never given me that type of future guidance, but He has given me all I have needed to know to do His will day by day.

He is your heavenly Father and you are His child if you have trusted Jesus as your Savior. Paul lovingly wrote to the Corinthian church, "All things belong to you" (1 Corinthians 3:21). I pondered these words for a year and asked God to open them up to me—"All things belong to you." I believe the meaning is that you will never lack anything that you need to know and do His will as you seek to love and obey your heavenly Father. Say with the psalmist, "But as for me, I trust in You, O Lord, I say, 'You are *my* God'" (Psalm 31:14, italics added).

Bob Richards, a former pole-vault champion, told a moving fictional story about a skinny young boy who loved football with all his heart. Practice after practice, he eagerly gave everything he had. But being half the size of the other boys, he got absolutely nowhere. At all the games, this hopeful athlete sat on the bench and hardly ever played. As a teenager he lived alone with his father, and the two of them had a very special relationship. Even though the son was always on the bench, his father was always in the stands cheering. He never missed a game.

This young man was still the smallest of the class when he entered high school. His father continued to encourage him but also made it very clear that he did not have to play football if he didn't want to. But the young man loved football and decided to hang in there. He was determined to try his best at every practice, and perhaps he'd get to play when he became a senior. All through high school he never missed a practice or a game, but he remained a bench warmer all four years. His faithful father was always in the stands, always with words of encouragement for him.

When the young man went to college, he decided to try out for the football team as a "walk-on." Everyone was sure he could never make the cut, but he did. The coach admitted that he kept him on the roster because he always put his heart and soul into every practice, and at the same time, he provided the other members with the spirit and hustle they badly needed. The news that he had survived the cut thrilled him so much that he rushed to the nearest phone and called his father and sent him season tickets for all the college games. His father shared his excitement. This persistent young athlete never missed practice during his four years of college, but again he never got to play in the game.

It was the end of his senior football season, and as he trotted onto the practice field a few days before the big play-off game, the coach met him with a telegram. The young man read the telegram and became silent. Swallowing hard, he mumbled to the coach, "My father died this morning. Is it all right if I miss practice today?" The coach put his arm gently around his shoulders and said, "Take the rest of the week off, son. And you don't even need to come back to the game on Saturday."

Saturday arrived, and the game was not going well. In the third quarter, when the team was ten points behind, a silent young man quietly slipped into the empty locker room and put on his football gear. As he ran onto the sidelines, the coach and his players were astounded to see their faithful teammate back so soon. "Coach, please let me play. I've just got to play today," said the young man. The coach pretended not to hear him. There was no way he wanted his worst player in this close play-off game. But the young man persisted, and finally, feeling sorry for the kid, the coach gave in.

"All right," he said, "you can go in." Before long, the coach, the players, and everyone in the stands could not believe their eyes. This little unknown who had never played before was doing everything right. The opposing team could not stop him. He ran, passed, blocked, and tackled like a star. His team began to triumph. The score was soon tied. In the closing seconds of the game, the kid intercepted a pass and ran all the way for the winning touchdown. The fans broke loose. His teammates hoisted him onto their shoulders. Such cheering you never heard!

Finally, after the stands had emptied and the team had showered and left the locker room, the coach noticed that the young man was sitting quietly in the corner all alone. The coach came to him and said, "Kid, I can't believe it. You were fantastic! Tell me what got into you? How did you do it?"

The young man looked at the coach with tears in his eyes and said, "Well, you knew my dad died, but did you remember that my dad was blind?" The young man swallowed hard, forced a smile, and said, "Dad came to all my games, but today was the first time he could see me play, and I wanted to show him I could do it!" Like the athlete's father, God is always there cheering for us as our "Abba Father." He's always reminding us to go on. He's even offering us His hand, for He knows what is best and is willing to give us what we need and not simply what we want. God has never missed a single game. What a joy to know that life is meaningful if lived for the Highest. Live for *Him,* for He's watching us in the game of life.

GOD IS SPIRIT

The truth that God is spirit and not able to be seen with the eye might seem like a limitation. You might think, *If only He would come to my home and just tell me what to do, whom to marry, which home to buy, or which school to attend, then it would be easy to do God's will.* Although He is invisible, He can be known by faith. Faith is the evidence or conviction of things not seen (Hebrews 11:1). Although He cannot be seen, He has been clearly revealed in the Lord Jesus Christ who did come to earth (John 1:18). In fact He can be known in such a way that although you have not seen Him, you can love Him, trust Him, and rejoice in Him (1 Peter 1:8).

In fact, the truth that God is spirit is a great help in experiencing God's will because He can live inside of you and satisfy your longings. Many people have a tendency to expect a person or a job to do for them what only God can do. Only God can fully satisfy the longings of your spirit.

I remember the wise words of Jim Sammons at our wedding, "Expectations destroy relationships." He humbly related this truth through his own experiences. Because he wanted to make his one-month wedding anniversary special, he went out and bought a gift that would endure over the lifetime of their marriage—a beautiful pink plastic rose. His wife took it, but she seemed less than enthusiastic when at the end of the second month of their marriage she received two more. When he gave her three a month later she exclaimed, "I don't like plastic roses." He expected her to be excited, and she expected him to realize that women like real roses. You and I cannot escape our longings. We can let them take us to Jesus, who promises to satisfy our thirst (John 7:37–39).

Because God is spirit, it is His will for us to worship Him in spirit and in truth (John 4:24). To worship God in spirit is to worship Him from the heart. It is expressed in the words of Psalm 40:8 which prophetically speaks of Jesus, "I delight to do Your will, O my God; Your Law is within my heart." I used to think that the epitome of Christian commitment was the willingness to give up one's plans and reluctantly obey God. But it is God's will to put an inner delight in our hearts to do His will. This is worshiping God in our spirits—that is a result of the filling of His Spirit (Ephesians 5:18–19).

It is God's will for us to worship Him not only in our spirits but also in truth. There may be different expressions of our worship, but it is always to be in accord with the truth of His revelation. We do not worship a God who is inconsistent but One who is faithful (2 Thessalonians 3:3). We do not worship a God who is insensitive to human need but One who is merciful (Ephesians 2:4). We do not worship a God who is tolerant of sin but One who is holy (1 Peter 1:16). If you make worshiping God in spirit and truth the top priority of your life, you will not miss His will.

GOD IS UNCHANGING

When God declares Himself immutable or unchanging, He is declaring His perfection. You see, God does not need to mature in any of His qualities. He could not possibly be wiser, holier, more truthful, more merciful, or more loving. Unlike us, He has no need for growth or improvement. He also does not need to add any additional qualities. Not only is He perfectly mature in all His attributes, but He also has all the qualities that compose a perfect person. Furthermore, He is not deteriorating or running out of any quality. He is not running out of love or power. When you see God provide for another person in special ways and you are tempted to be jealous, remember that God is not using up His goodness. He does not have any less capacity to bless and provide for you. After you have trusted God and seen His work on your behalf, have you ever felt anxious the next time you were faced with a new situation? God will not run out of faithfulness or power or whatever His children need to do His will.

God alone is perfect. This helps us in our pursuit of the will of God. In this sense of God's perfection there is not a perfect job, a perfect husband or wife, a perfect house, a perfect church, or a perfect vacation. God is to be supremely sought over all of His gracious provisions. He is able to give "perfect" gifts in that they will fulfill His "perfect will" for us in the midst of a sinful world (James 1:17; Romans 12:2).

Because God is unchangeably truthful, His Word can be trusted. I remember hearing about an individual who had attended the same seminary I did a few years before me. It was the second seminary he had attended. He had studied a particular theology at his previous school that even liberals no longer believed. He returned to seminary to learn a better, more accurate theology. Men's ideas are very changeable, but God's are not. The prophet Isaiah said, "The grass withers, the flower fades, but the word of our God stands forever" (Isaiah 40:8). God's Word stands forever because it is backed by His unchanging character. His promises can be trusted, for "not one word has failed of all His good promise" (1 Kings 8:56).

I married later in my life, at the age of thirty-six. It was God's plan for me to finish all my college, seminary, and doctoral programs, and even to teach for eight and a half years before marrying. One day I was talking to God about that area of my life and telling Him what I was trusting Him for, when I was overwhelmed with a barrage of accusing thoughts. The accusations that screamed at me were, "You're so unreasonable, and you're just unrealistic. You can't trust God to answer your need for companionship." At that moment Ephesians 3:20 was brought to my mind. It speaks of God as the One "who is able to do far more abundantly beyond all that we ask or think." For years I stood on that promise. Many times I said to the Lord, "I don't know what You have for me in this area of my life, but I believe it is abundantly above all I can ask or think." When God sent Penny into my life as my wife, she was the answer to that promise.

In my life, there are still many areas that are mysteries to me. But we know it is God's will for us to look to Him and His unchanging promises. Dr. Warren Wiersbe once told how a listener to his radio program had written an encouraging poem to him. It has blessed me and many others. "Yesterday God helped me. Today He will do the same. How long will it last? Forever, praise His name!"

God can be trusted with the tomorrows of our lives. There have been times when God was taking care of me abundantly in the present, but I lost my joy by focusing on the uncertainty of the future. We need to heed Christ's wise words, "Do not be anxious for tomorrow; for tomorrow will care for itself. Each day has enough trouble of its own" (Matthew 6:34).

It is God's will for you to build your life around

Him who does not change. What a kind command is found in the words of Exodus 20:3, "You shall have no other gods before Me." Although we are desperately in need of other people, it is not God's will to make another human the center of our lives. Although God gives us various jobs and positions, all of this can so easily change. The Lord even encouraged wealthy people not to "fix their hope on the uncertainty of riches, but on God, who richly supplies us with all things to enjoy" (1 Timothy 6:17). The great German reformer Martin Luther, who was so mightily used in church history, was asked one day, "Where will you be if all your followers leave you?" He replied, "I'll be right in the very hands of God."

We are also to "be imitators of God." Ephesians 5:1–2 applies this phrase to walking in love, and a key aspect of love is imitating God's consistency and faithfulness. If you seek God's will, you need to examine the commitments and vows that you have made in your life. If you have made marriage vows, one of the most important things in God's will for you is to be true to those vows. In fact, the answer to the question, "*How* can I best fulfill my marriage vows?" may give you some discernment into God's will.

It is God's will for you to be faithful to your responsibilities. In regard to employment, it is a safe rule of thumb to stay at one's present job until God makes it clear to change. If a person is always flirting with change, it may be that God is more concerned about teaching that person contentment than giving him or her a new job.

GOD IS ETERNAL

"Even from everlasting to everlasting, You are God" declared Moses in Psalm 90:2. When we put our trust in the Lord Jesus Christ for our salvation, we enter into a relationship with the eternal God. Part of knowing and doing God's will is understanding God's priorities for you. I was struck by the phrase in Romans 1:23 that speaks of exchanging the glory of the *incorruptible* God for that which is *corruptible*. When man foolishly rejects God's revelation, he no longer builds his life around that which cannot be destroyed.

As I pondered this verse I asked myself, "How many things does God's Word declare to be incorruptible?" As I went to a concordance I noted five distinct uses of the Greek word *aphthartos,* which is translated "incorruptible" in Romans 1:23. God declares the following five things to be incorruptible or imperishable.

1. God Himself—Romans 1:23; 1 Timothy 1:17
2. God's Word—1 Peter 1:23
3. Resurrected Bodies—1 Corinthians 15:53
4. Heavenly Rewards—1 Corinthians 9:25; 1 Peter 1:4
5. Enduring Effects of Godly Character—1 Peter 3:4

As you pursue God's will, you can develop a philosophy of life around these five things. We are to build our lives around God and His Word and trust Him to build godly character in our lives as we live in the hope of being rewarded by Him in our new resurrected bodies. The character that we allow God to build in our lives is declared to be imperishable.

Jesus put a great emphasis on encouraging His followers to live for eternity. You can look up the following Scripture texts and note how these principles flow out of them.

- An eternal gain is better than temporary gain (Matthew 6:19–20).
- A temporary loss is better than an eternal loss (Matthew 5:29–30).
- Any sacrifice for Christ's name will be rewarded for all eternity (Matthew 19:29–30).
- Any action done independent of Christ will result in nothing of eternal value (John 15:5).

If we examined our schedules and our checkbooks, would they reveal God's eternal priorities? God encourages us in our pursuit of His will to take these priorities into account.

The truth of God's eternality also provides a very valuable perspective for us. First of all, we need perspective in regard to who we are. The New Testament declares every Christian to be:

- A citizen of heaven (Philippians 3:20)
- An alien and a stranger on this earth (1 Peter 2:11)
- An ambassador for Christ (2 Corinthians 5:20)

You may take a walk through a neighborhood and wrongly conclude that life is about buying cars and houses, since much of a person's time and energy goes to making money to obtain these possessions. There is nothing wrong with trusting God to provide the transportation and housing you need to do His will, but we are merely aliens since this present earth is not the place of our permanent residence. We are here on temporary assignment to represent Christ to the world.

Another thing that the truth of our eternal God can put into perspective is time. After surrendering my life to Christ, time took on a new meaning. As a college student, I went to the chairman of the department of management and asked him for permission to do an independent study on time management from a Christian's perspective. He graciously gave me permission, and it was a tremendous help to me. I realized that time with God is not truly *spent*, but rather *invested*. The value of time took on new meaning. Scripture has more to say about time than I imagined.

We all live under the command of God to make the most of our time (Ephesians 5:16) and all are given a specific amount of time on this earth to do His will. Jesus felt this deeply as He exclaimed, "We must work the works of Him who sent Me as long as it is day; night is coming when no one can work" (John 9:4). In

God's loving and all-wise plan, we have all the time we need to accomplish His will for us. Jesus said these amazing words to the Father at the end of His life: "I glorified You on the earth, having accomplished the work which You have given Me to do" (John 17:4).

At the end of his life, Moses wrote this prayer: "So teach us to number our days, that we may present to You a heart of wisdom" (Psalm 90:12). We can live with the illusion that we will live forever on this earth. God, however, has given us a deadline to consider. As a general rule, man lives about seventy or eighty years, according to Psalm 90:10. Some of us may have a much shorter life and some may have a longer one, but this is the general rule. I remember Dr. Bruce Waltke encouraging people to literally compute the probable number of days of their lives. You can do this by multiplying seventy (or eighty) by 365.25. Then subtract the days you have already lived, which can be computed by multiplying your age by 365.25 and adding the days past your birthday. I applied this idea to my life more than twenty years ago, and every day since then I have entered a new number at the top of my Day-Timer, a number which gets closer to zero from the maximum probable lifespan of 25,567 or 29,220 days. The reality that hits me is that I am dying *and coming closer to my own day of accounting before the Lord.*

The diligence to use our time wisely to do God's will should not be accompanied by a hurried spirit. John Wesley, who was known for his diligence, said, "Although I am always in haste, I am never in a hurry. I never do more than I can do except with perfect calmness of spirit." God wants to teach us to live with a trust in His timing. When Jesus came to earth He came in "the fullness of the time" (Galatians 4:4). When He died, He died "at the right time" (Romans 5:6). God's perspective of time is *far different from ours*. He can do in one day what you may think it would take a thousand years to do, if ever (2 Peter 3:8). The pursuit of God's will often includes waiting. Although waiting is obnoxious to the flesh, it is an important thing to learn in doing God's will.

A Canaanite woman came to Jesus one day and cried out for His merciful help for her daughter. Jesus did not even answer her! She persistently shouted at His disciples and then came back to Jesus to inquire of His help. This time He seemed to be a little hard on her as He stated, "It is not good to take the children's bread and throw it to the dogs" (Matthew 15:26). Her continual persistence was rewarded with not only the healing of her daughter *but one of the four recorded compliments of Jesus issued in the Gospels* (v. 28).

Dr. T. W. Hunt once remarked concerning this passage that God many times wants to give us more than we know to ask. Jesus' silence (Matthew 15:23) and apparent harshness (Matthew 15:26) are not to be taken as His indifference to our requests as we wait on Him. He wants to give us His will, and He wants to give us Himself.

The truth of God's eternality also helps to put in perspective the trials of our life. Look at these passages from Scripture that highlight the importance of having an eternal perspective on life:

> *"For I consider that the sufferings of this present time are not worthy to be compared with the glory that is to be revealed to us." (Romans 8:18)*

> *"For momentary, light affliction is producing for us an eternal weight of glory far beyond all comparison, while we look not at the things which are seen, but at the things which are not seen; for the things which are seen are temporal, but the things which are not seen are eternal." (2 Corinthians 4:17–18)*

> *"In this you greatly rejoice, even though now for a little while, if necessary, you have been distressed by various trials, so that the proof of your faith, being more precious than gold which is perishable, even though tested by fire, may be found to result in praise and glory and honor at the revelation of Jesus Christ." (1 Peter 1:6–7)*

Without these perspectives of our future hope, our trials can easily leave us disillusioned as we seek God's will. This was the case of the psalmist until he gained a perspective of God's future judgment (Psalm 73:17). All that will matter when we stand before the judgment seat of Christ is how we expressed our love and faith in obedience to Him (1 Corinthians 13:1–3; 2 Corinthians 5:10).

The truth of God's eternality is a help in giving us both the priority and perspective that is needed to do God's will. It also can give us a sense of anticipation. A believer in Christ can anticipate experiencing these four things for all eternity.

1. *Comfort:* "Now may our Lord Jesus Christ Himself and God our Father, who has loved us and given us *eternal comfort* and good hope by grace, comfort and strengthen your hearts in every good work and word" (2 Thessalonians 2:16–17, italics added). Think of experiencing God's comfort for all eternity! Do not let the personal pursuit of comfort in this life be a hindrance to pursuing the will of God. We can trust God to comfort us in our afflictions in this life, but this is only a foretaste of what we will experience for all eternity. One day I spilled a cup of coffee all over myself on an airplane. I asked, *I wonder what good is going to come out of this?* I can still recall the comfort that came when a kind person took an interest in me and told me what would get the coffee stain out of my shirt. Live for God, for He can care for us even in our clumsiness!

2. *Joy:* "In Your presence is fullness of joy; in Your right hand there are pleasures forever" (Psalm 16:11). God has joys for us to experience for all eternity. We should not be deceived into thinking that pursuing God's will will cause us to miss out on something.

3. *Vindication:* "Truthful lips will be established forever, but a lying tongue is only for a moment"
(Proverbs 12:19). You may have refused to cheat
on an exam and not gotten as good a grade as
one who had been dishonest. God's grade for
you in heaven will be higher. You may have
been honest on your income tax and paid more
than if you had been dishonest. You clearly did
God's will and will be grateful for all eternity.
There is no better time than now to clear your
conscience of any falsehood in your life. "There
is nothing covered up that will not be revealed,
and hidden that will not be known" (Luke
12:2).

4. *Praise:* "The Creator, who is blessed forever"
(Romans 1:25). You can anticipate praising God
forever. It is God's will for you to begin today.

Keeping your eyes and mind focused on the eternal Person of the Lord Jesus Christ and His loving
works will help you understand His will for you. Even
if you don't know everything (and you won't), you can
be confident that when you seek His will on a particular matter, your understanding of His eternal nature is
the right starting point to identify the paths He wants
you to follow.

Chapter   Six

◆

The Power
of God

A lmost everyone is familiar with the tragic story of the great ocean liner *Titanic*. Although it doesn't rank as the greatest catastrophe at sea in terms of lives lost, it is unquestionably the most famous, its details recounted in myriad books, movies, and television documentaries. Some are fact, others more fictitious.

Perhaps the quality about the Titanic's sinking that serves to capture our attention most is the supreme confidence that its builders, owners, and passengers held about the ship's invulnerability. "Unsinkable" was the pronouncement of the White Star Line, the ship's owners, who had built the largest, most sophisticated ship that had ever been commissioned. As she prepared for her maiden voyage from Liverpool to New

York in April 1912, some declared boldly, "Even God Himself could not sink her."

The Titanic can help us focus on the contrast of the power of our sovereign Lord with our own best efforts. When we look at the Titanic disaster in its simplest assessment, the best and brightest of man's efforts was demolished in two short hours by a giant ice cube. If all the powers in the world—nuclear, solar, hydro-electric, magnetic, satanic, etc.—were put together, they would not begin to measure up to the omnipotence of God.

But God's power is really not about upsetting our own carefully planned apple carts. His power is a reminder to us of who is really in charge of this world. And more important, it's a reminder that we can benefit from His power when our whole heart is completely His and we rely on His character (2 Chronicles 16:7–9).

Besides being a person, as we learned in the last chapter, God is all-powerful and all-knowing. In fact, He is the source of power and knowledge. Our own limited power and knowledge has its origins in our heavenly Father. Samson didn't slay a thousand Philistines with the jawbone of an ass by himself. God used Samson to demonstrate His power to unbelievers. The donkey didn't speak to Balaam in Numbers 22:28–30 because of a hidden ability awakened. God gave her the ability and knowledge to use gifts not present in animals. Even home-run hitters Mark McGwire and Sammy Sosa owe their abilities to God. Recognizing this, however, is another matter. The more we recognize this aspect of God's character, the closer we will come to understanding how He works in our own lives and how we might come to know His will for us.

GOD IS ALL-KNOWING

Psalm 139:1–6 says,

> *O Lord, You have searched me and known me. You know when I sit down and when I rise up; You understand my thought from afar. You scrutinize my path and my lying down, and are intimately acquainted with all my ways. Even before there is a word on my tongue, behold, O Lord, You know it all. You have enclosed me behind and before, and laid Your hand upon me. Such knowledge is too wonderful for me; it is too high, I cannot attain to it.*

As you seek God's will, you can worship a God who knows all the possibilities. He knows what *could* happen as well as what *would* happen if any given possibility did happen. He knows all about your past, present, and future. Let such knowledge lead you to a greater awe of Him. We should never lose sight of the forgiveness of One who knows every thought, word, and deed of our life! Let the truth of His omniscience, His perfect knowledge, challenge you to live openly before Him, and seek to live in agreement with Him as you pursue His will.

Wherever you are today, God knows your needs, your trials, and your opposition. He even knows a solution to the problems that perplex you. I have tried to teach my children to pray for the things they lose around the house. God has honored this many times. I also remember frantically looking for something one day only to have one of my sons say to me, "Daddy, have you prayed for it?" I stopped and prayed at that moment. Oh, the lessons that our children can teach us!

When my oldest son, Will, was five years old, we were visiting my mother in Montgomery, Alabama. Will loved baseball and desperately wanted some cleats. His mother had told him to pray for some. When Penny was visiting a resale shop to look for some clothes, Will went straight to look at the shoes. There was one pair of cleats, and they were his size. This was worth a thousand lectures on God's omniscience. He knows our homes, our addresses, and our needs as we seek His will.

Pursuing God's will is a continual process because God desires to build a relationship with you. He could just drop a piece of paper to you each day that outlines what He wants for that day. You might have direction, but you would miss the greater prize of a relationship with Him.

God knows all the needs of the world, and He also knows your talents and strengths. He knows every possibility of where to place you and with whom to place you. When God's people were in bondage in Egypt, they cried to God to deliver them. God heard this cry and had in fact been preparing a deliverer for forty years. In God's time, their cry for help was answered through Moses. God is preparing you. He knows all the needs of the world, and He knows how and where to place you to meet some of those needs.

Since God's will is exactly what we would desire if we knew all the facts, we need to remember that God is the only one who knows all the facts. A pastor once said that he and the other elders had agreed that a certain individual should be invited to join the staff of the church. The board asked the pastor to have lunch with the man. In the process of the conversation over lunch, the pastor had an incredible heaviness in his spirit about bringing up the topic of the staff position, and he ended the lunch without doing so. He humbly reported back to the board the experience of the lunch. Shortly afterward, a damaging issue about this man surfaced that none of the elders was aware of. The board worshiped God and praised Him for not allowing this to surface in their church after the man had been hired.

GOD IS EVERYWHERE

Psalm 139:7–12 says,

> *Where can I go from Your Spirit? Or where can I flee from Your presence? If I ascend to heaven, You are there; if I make my bed in Sheol, behold, You are there. If I take the wings of the dawn, if I dwell in the remotest part of the sea, even there Your hand will lead me, and Your right*

hand will lay hold of me. If I say, "Surely the darkness will
overwhelm me, and the light around me will be night,"
even the darkness is not dark to You, and the night is as
bright as the day. Darkness and light are alike to You.

It is accurate to say that God is everywhere but not
everywhere in the same way. The Scriptures speak of
God's presence in at least four ways. First, God is
everywhere so that Paul could even say to a group of
unbelievers, "In Him we live and move and exist" (Acts
17:28). Can you imagine being with somebody all the
time and not being in harmony with him or her? The
first step of God's will for a person is to trust Jesus
Christ and establish peace with God. Second, Scripture also speaks of special manifestations of God's
presence such as His being in the tabernacle and in the
temple. Now God declares His people, both individu-
ally and corporately, to be His temple (1 Corinthians
6:19; Ephesians 2:21). Paul's words "To be absent from
the body and to be at home with the Lord" (2 Corinthians 5:8) reveal a third way that the Scriptures
speak of God's presence. His thought is akin to Jesus'
words, "Our Father who is in heaven" (Matthew 6:9).

The final way that Scripture speaks of God's presence is the cultivation of a conscious enjoyment of His
presence. Have you ever been in a prayer meeting and
heard someone pray, "Lord, I pray that you would be
with that person"? Have you also heard someone else
say, "Don't pray God would be with that person, because God is everywhere"? God is certainly every-

where, but the apostle Paul prayed, "Now the God of peace be with you all" (Romans 15:33). Perhaps we should be more cautious in rebuking the one praying and know what we mean when we pray it.

It is God's will that you experience His presence in your life. An unknown author wrote, "God is for us— that is good. God is with us—that is better. God is in us—that is best." The Spirit permanently indwells every Christian who puts his or her faith in the finished work of Christ, but He can be grieved through sin and quenched through disobedience. God desires that you develop an enjoyment of His presence as expressed in Psalm 16:8, "I have set the Lord continually before me; because He is at my right hand, I will not be shaken." One of the greatest compliments in the Bible was spoken to Abraham, "God is with you in all that you do" (Genesis 21:22).

An evangelist once exclaimed to his audience, "I keep praying that God will come to this church." A friend of mine believes that in many places God has disciplined His church by withdrawing His manifest presence. Do you not long for an unbeliever to come to your home or your church and fall down in repentance and worship and declare that God is certainly in this place (1 Corinthians 14:24–25)?

When David Livingstone, who had been a missionary in Africa, received an honorary degree from Glasgow University, he rose to speak. He looked quite gaunt. His left arm, which had been crushed by a lion, hung helplessly by his side. He announced his resolve to return to Africa without any hesitation and with great joy. As he spoke he stated, "Would you like me to tell you what supported me through the years of exile among a people whose language I could not understand and whose attitude toward me was always uncertain and often hostile? It was this, 'Lo, I am with you always, even to the end of the age!' On these words I staked everything. They never failed."[1] It is God's will for you and me to cultivate the companionship of the Lord's holy presence through a life of trust and obedience.

Is not the central thrust of God's will to glorify Him? It honors people when others acknowledge their presence, and it greatly distresses them to be ignored or offended. How would you like to be invited to spend time with a close friend for a day, but never be acknowledged by the person? Cultivating a conscious enjoyment of God's presence brings great honor to Him and great benefit to you. Revel in the amazing promise of never having to be alone (Hebrews 13:5)! Think of who is with you—your Creator, your Father, Protector, Friend, Lover, and He who is perfect love, power, and wisdom.

A young man came up to me one day after I had spoken on this theme and exclaimed, "I'm not so sure I want to know that God is with me at all times." He was worried that God might hinder some of his own plans for his life. That comment revealed a failure to recognize the way Scripture describes God's presence.

- Place of satisfaction—Psalm 65:4
- Place of strength and beauty—Psalm 96:6
- Place of blessing—2 Samuel 6:11
- Place of insight and perspective—Exodus 33:9–11; Psalm 73:17
- Place of stability and joy—Psalm 16:8–9
- Place of success and enablement—Genesis 39:1–3, 21–23
- Place of refreshment—Acts 3:19.

This young man did not know what he was rejecting. Certainly God's presence is an exhortation to cleanse our life from sin. Would an employee steal before the eyes of his employer? Would one commit adultery before the eyes of his or her spouse? All sin is before the holy and living presence of God. The exhortation to draw near to God is followed by the command to cleanse and purify our lives (James 4:8). However, God is the most reconcilable Person with whom you will ever have a relationship. It is His will for you to know the joy of His presence.

Let us close our reflections on God's presence with one practical point on the will of God. It is not God's will for you to live with a hurried spirit. One of the most unusual days of my life occurred in my early years of teaching. Dr. George Sweeting, who was then the president of Moody Bible Institute, was deeply moved by the chapel speaker that morning. He rose from his chair to the pulpit and said, "Classes will be cancelled tomorrow. They will meet, but only to pray." This happened in the middle of a busy fall semester. The students got excited, and so did I. I began to talk to the Lord. I asked, "Lord, what do You want me to do with this day? Do You want me to fast?" It did not seem that the Lord was impressed with any of my ideas.

I arose the next morning and ate a good breakfast in a restaurant right across from the train station. When I was single I used to visit such places quite often. They probably thought I died when I got married! As I got on the train I sensed God's leading to put down all of my studies and be still in the Lord's presence. I did not even think the Lord wanted me to talk very much at school. I led my classes in prayer with as few words of instruction as possible and then went home that afternoon. If you had seen me and asked me what I did that day I would have had to reply, "Nothing." I am sure you would not have been impressed.

I entered a restaurant before I got on the train and ate supper. And there a waitress told me something that had never been said to me. She said it not once, but three times. She exclaimed, "I go all over this restaurant and I sense hurry and rush, but I come to your booth and I sense peace." I felt like God was trying to knock me over the head to teach me a lesson. It was as if He said, "If I ever order you to slow down even from your efforts of serving Me, realize that it will bear great spiritual fruit."

Is your life too hurried? It is God's will to develop in you the spirit of Mary so that you can enjoy the presence of Christ (Luke 10:38–42). Do you need to learn what I did, that you can accomplish more working six days a week than seven? What is your plan for your Sabbath rest? God will never give you so much to do that He will not give you time to cultivate a conscious enjoyment of Him.

GOD IS WISE

God is to be worshiped as "the only wise God" (Romans 16:27) and to be praised because of His great desire to share His wisdom with you. It is God's will that you become wise.

What is wisdom?

Perhaps it is best not to limit this to a single definition, although "the ability to see life from God's point of view" is a very helpful one. James 1:2 gives the proper response to trials when they are seen from God's viewpoint. Wisdom is also the ability to select the best goals for one's life and the best means to reach those goals. In other words, it is the ability to know where to go and how to get there.

One year I had a prayer burden in my heart, and the only way I knew how to express it was in the words, "Lord, help me to aim my life at the right things." I had a concern that I might aim my life at the wrong thing and perhaps even achieve it but later find out that it was not the thing about which God's heart was most concerned. This was my most heartfelt prayer request of that year. I did not know enough at that time to call it that, but it was a petition for wisdom. I believe that one thing that came out of that year was an emphasis on the character of God.

God's wisdom may also be defined as the skill of living life before God. The Hebrew word for wisdom, *hakmah,* speaks of a skill. For example, the book of Proverbs is designed to give us skill in living. Just as people can have skills in areas such as carpentry, they can learn skill in using the tongue, handling money, relating to different kinds of people, parenting, friendship, and marriage. Growing in His wisdom is a great key in the experience of God's will.

The Value of God's Wisdom

Proverbs 3:13–15 says, "How blessed is the man who finds wisdom and the man who gains understanding. For her profit is better than the profit of silver and her gain better than fine gold. She is more precious than jewels; and nothing you desire compares with her."

Can you seriously say that you agree with God's estimation, "Nothing you desire compares with her"? What is your desire in regard to God's will? I remember what mine was one hot summer day. God had put a young lady on my heart who eventually became my wife. That desire was very concrete. I decided to use this desire to prompt me to pray that God would teach me the value of wisdom. Every time I thought of her, I would use the thought as a reminder to pray for God to teach me the value of wisdom. I would say, "Lord, Your wisdom is more important to me than Penny. In my mind I can accept this, but let Your truth grip my emotions." We are not to live by our emotions, but God's truth is to refocus our emotions on the Lord's values.

If I had had two special gift boxes, but allowed you to pick only one, which would you choose? Your natural curiosity would probably ask me what was in each box. If I told you Box #1 contained all you desire and Box #2 contained wisdom, which would you choose? God's Word says that there is no comparison between the value of the two. Without God's wisdom you could have all you desire and make a mess of it. God's wisdom is the most valuable gift.

Gaining God's Wisdom

The following is an attempt to summarize the teaching of Scripture on how to become wise.

- Recognize your need for it. As we pursue God's will we must continually realize that we are sheep who need a Shepherd (see Jeremiah 10:23). For this reason wisdom is given to the humble (Proverbs 11:2) and to those who first admit they are foolish (1 Corinthians 3:18).
- Recognize its value and desire it above all else. Although Solomon did not always live by the wisdom God gave him, he did certainly give us an example worth following in his petition to God. Second Chronicles 1:8–12 says,

> Solomon said to God, . . . "Now, O Lord God, Your promise to my father David is fulfilled, for You have made me king over a people as numerous as the dust of the earth. Give me now wisdom and knowledge, that I may go out and come in before this people, for who can rule this great people of Yours?" God said to Solomon, "Because you had this in mind, and did not ask for riches, wealth or honor, or the life of those who hate you, nor have you even asked for long life, but you have asked for yourself wisdom and knowledge that you may rule My people over whom I have made you king, wisdom and knowledge have been granted to you. And I will give you riches and wealth and honor, such as none of the kings who were before you has possessed nor those who will come after you."

- Cultivate a fear of God. The fear of God is the beginning of true knowledge (Proverbs 1:7) and wisdom (Proverbs 9:10) and gives one the courage to reject evil and do right. Fear of God is a basic need of mankind (Romans 3:18), and it can be achieved only by a balanced understanding of the true God (Proverbs 2:5).
- Diligently and prayerfully study Scripture. Satan has a counterfeit wisdom (James 3:15), but God's wisdom will always be in harmony with the principles of God's Word (Deuteronomy 4:5–6).
- Ask God for it in prayer. God can give us His wisdom in the midst of our trial (James 1:5), and

it is His will to give us wisdom in our inner being (Psalm 51:6).

- Fellowship with wise people. The people with whom we have intimate associations will have a profound influence on our lives. One way to become wise is to associate with wise people (Proverbs 13:20).
- Maintain a teachable spirit, and be willing to accept rebuke. A person's response to correction reveals a lot about him (Proverbs 9:8–9, 12:15).
- Maintain innocence concerning evil. You will not become wise by experimenting with wrong philosophies and evil but by avoiding them (Romans 16:19).
- Trust in God and not in yourself. It is foolish to trust in your own heart (Proverbs 28:26), but wise to live under the control of the Spirit (Ephesians 5:15, 18).
- Let the pursuit of wisdom be a joy. Although the foolish can find amusement in wickedness, the discerning person finds his satisfaction in wisdom (Proverbs 10:23).

The pursuit of God's wisdom will inevitably lead you to the experience of God's will.

GOD IS ALL-POWERFUL

"I know that You can do all things, and that no purpose of Yours can be thwarted" (Job 42:2).

As we seek God's will, we will have to learn to lean on God, due to our own inadequacy. He alone can make us adequate (2 Corinthians 2:16; 3:6). Although training and preparation for our vocations are an important aspect of God's plan, they are never to be the object of our trust (Psalm 33:16–17; Proverbs 21:31). Whatever makes you feel inadequate from God's perspective is the greatest thing you have going for you. One of the most serious rebukes ever given to God's people is chastisement for their attitude of self-sufficiency. Revelation 3:15–16 states, "I know your deeds, that you are neither cold nor hot; I wish that you were cold or hot. So because you are lukewarm, and neither hot nor cold, I will spit you out of My mouth." God rebukes our self-sufficiency, but not our admission of our need for Him. For this reason, a wise prayer is, "Lord, show me what it means to allow you to be strong in my weakness" (see 2 Corinthians 12:9–10).

It is also important to remember that the Lord can open doors of opportunities that no one can shut (Revelation 3:8). An open door does not necessarily mean that there will not be opposition, as can be seen in 1 Corinthians 16:9. However, you can trust God to deal with opposition. The ultimate opposition we have is the spiritual forces that oppose us. Such opposition seeks to hinder us from doing the will of God (1 Thessalonians 2:18). However, you are to focus on God, who is greater than all your opposition, because He is for you (Romans 8:31). If you are interested in another person and desire to marry him or her, you have to trust God to open that person's heart. It is not totally up to you. You have probably heard the story of the boy who went to the girl and said, "God told me to marry you," to which the girl replied, "He hasn't told me yet."

Billy Stroud ran a small accounting firm in Houston, Texas. He sought to live his life and operate his business with the highest integrity. One time he needed to make a very difficult decision in order to maintain complete honesty, and many people told him that such a decision would ruin his business. God used Hebrews 13:6 to give him the courage to do what he knew was right. Hebrews 13:5–6 says, "Let your character be free from the love of money, being content with what you have; for He Himself has said, 'I will never desert you, nor will I ever forsake you,' so that we confidently say, 'The Lord is my helper, I will not be afraid. *What will man do to me?*'" (italics added). He honored the Lord in his decision, his business continued to thrive, and he focused on God's power and not being snared by the fear of men (Proverbs 29:25).

Every client who went to Billy's office saw a strange-looking Greek word behind his desk. It was the word *Tetelestai,* which is translated "It is finished!" (John 19:30). As people asked about this plaque he explained the Gospel to many. He trusted the power of God in his life.

As you seek God's will and as you do it, you will continually find yourself asking the question, What is my part and what is God's? Doing His will does require "labor," but we are to "labor, striving according to His power" (Colossians 1:29). There is a vast difference between laboring and laboring according to His power. Both will tire you out, but one will weary you much sooner, and the other will leave you inwardly refreshed in the midst of your weariness. Put your finger on Colossians 1:29 and ask Him to make this real in your experience. Letting Him teach you this truth is a most precious part of His will for you. "A Christian is a person who, when getting to the end of his rope, ties a knot and determines to hang on, realizing that the human extremity now becomes God's opportunity" (Author Unknown).

GOD IS SOVEREIGN

"My frame was not hidden from You, when I was made in secret, and skillfully wrought in the depths of the earth; Your eyes have seen my unformed substance; and in Your book were all written the days that were ordained for me, when as yet there was not one of them" (Psalm 139:15–16).

That God is sovereign means that He is never out of control. The fact that He has given to man the capacity to make responsible decisions does not limit His sovereignty; it magnifies it! God's will can be looked at in these three ways:

His preceptive will: This is what God desires. For example, He desires all to be saved (1 Timothy 2:4).

His permissive will: This is what God permits. He permits people to reject Him.

His providential will: This is what happens as God overrules evil to accomplish His purposes: For example, God overruled the greatest evil that ever happened to make salvation available to the whole world (Matthew 21:42; Acts 2:23).

Another example is in regard to the unity of His church. In His preceptive will, He desires unity (Ephesians 4:1–3), but in His permissive will, He allows strife and discord. He overrules this disunity to accomplish His purposes and allow the true peacemakers to be known (1 Corinthians 11:19). God's preceptive will guides us into His desires, and His providential will gives us a ground of trust. If it were possible for God to be out of control for one minute, you could not trust Him, for He could not give you a promise like Romans 8:28!

As long as you live on this earth you will have people in authority over you in the church, the workplace, the home, or the government. Whereas God is ultimately in control of every authority (Proverbs 21:1, Romans 13:1), this does not necessarily mean that He is pleased with all authority. Every authority will answer to God for how it used its power (cf. Colossians 4:1). Every employer will answer to God for how he paid his employees (cf. Malachi 3:5), and every government leader is accountable for how he served his people.

Stephen Olford is a dear man of God who has done much international travel and has frequently met dignitaries and government leaders. He has often respectfully said something like this, "Sir, I know you are a busy man, but could I have a word of prayer with you?" His prayers have been used by God to speak to leaders' consciences and remind them of their accountability to God. All of us need to learn to submit to those in authority, respectfully appeal to them, and obey God's clear instruction to pray for them (1 Timothy 2:1–2). Perhaps if we took time to pray for our authorities when we are tempted to grumble and criticize them, our lives would be more in harmony with God's preceptive will.

Because God is sovereign we must recognize that all we have comes from God. "For who regards you as superior? And what do you have that you did not receive? But if you did receive it, why do you boast as if you had not received it?" (1 Corinthians 4:7).

> *So David blessed the Lord in the sight of all the assembly; and David said, "Blessed are You, O Lord God of Israel our father, forever and ever. Yours, O Lord, is the greatness and the power and the glory and the victory and the majesty, indeed everything that is in the heavens and the earth; Yours is the dominion, O Lord, and You exalt Yourself as head over all. Both riches and honor come from You, and You rule over all, and in Your hand is power and might; and it lies in Your hand to make great and to strengthen everyone." (1 Chronicles 29:10–12)*

Every talent or ability, opportunity or resource we have is a gift of God. Pride is attempting to take credit for what God has given us. When we are critical we are attempting to set ourselves up as sovereign, and when we are discontent we may be rebelling against His sovereign hand in our life. We need to recognize that we are accountable to God for all we have, and we are to be stewards of what God has given to us.

As you seek God's will you can do so with the comfort of "all things working together for good" that enables you to maintain a confident trust in God. Although you may have heard this verse quoted in a trite way, I'm sure you would hate to have a God who could not give us this comfort. To be sure we do need to marry it to Romans 12:15, which encourages us not only to rejoice with those who rejoice, but also to weep with those who weep. When my oldest son, Will, was three he ran to his six-month-old brother who had fallen down the stairs and was crying uncontrollably. As Will began to cry loudly with Michael, his mommy instructed him not to weep but rather to try to calm Michael down. He replied, "But Mommy, God says to weep with those who weep." He may have missed the point, but perhaps we empathize too little.

There is a comfort not only in knowing that God knows the future but also in agreeing with the psalmist and saying, "My times are in Your hand" (Psalm 31:15). This comfort can sustain us in the midst of uncertainty, confusion, and even the pain of processing the past. Every time I recalled a particular unpleasant situation, just the thought of it drained my energy. I took out a 3 x 5 card one day and began to write down the good that God had brought out of that painful experience. That exercise was very therapeutic for my soul.

An individual who grew up with an alcoholic father was being exhorted to thank God for her dad, who had not provided for her. She was hit with the idea that she had the capacity to be extra grateful for her husband, who did stay sober and work. Do not misunderstand what I am saying. I am not saying that pain is not pain! I am saying that the perspective of a sovereign God is the only framework in which to heal and proceed to do the will of God.

In every aspect of our lives, we must acknowledge that God is supreme and all-encompassing. There is no place that He hasn't created and no true knowledge that does not stem from His mind. This acknowledgment of Him in all our ways leads us to the experience of His will (Proverbs 3:5–6). We have been placed here to glorify Him, to affirm His glorious character that He has revealed. This is the greatest achievement in God's will. When we accept this higher purpose, we can love Him in our present circumstances as we trust Him to make our future clear. In the process, every child of God can enjoy the benefit of His amazing love, which is as plentiful as He is powerful.

NOTE

1. Stephen F. Olford, *Going Places with God* (Wheaton, Ill.: Victor, 1983), 20.

◆

Chapter Seven

The Perfection of God

A aron Ramsey sat on the bench in the locker room after the game reflecting on his great fortune. He had just pitched a no-hitter. In only his second year in the major leagues, he had accomplished what most pitchers only dream of doing: pitching a perfect game. He had come close in college and the minors, but never made it. He had now grasped the Holy Grail of baseball.

As the last batter for the other team watched in awe as the curve ball whizzed past him for the third strike, the stadium had erupted in mad euphoria. Aaron was carried off the field on the shoulders of his teammates, while fans screamed, "Aaron, Aaron!" Now that the interviews and the backslapping were over, Aaron paused to relish his accomplishment while changing clothes to leave the stadium. He was on top of the world. Everything was perfect. He was perfect. The sportswriters were already comparing him to the greats of the game. "Another Sandy Koufax," said one. "The next Nolan Ryan," another had written.

As he walked out of the locker room, one of the janitorial staff took time to congratulate Aaron. "Great game, Mr. Ramsey. Do it again on Thursday."

Aaron smiled and thanked the man as he left. Out in the parking lot, though, the impact of the janitor's comments dawned on him. "Do it again on Thursday." Pitch another perfect game? Impossible. Back-to-back no-hitters? He'd be lucky to do it again in his career, much less continuously. Suddenly, his feelings of perfection and joy abandoned him. His head slumped as he trudged to his car, sensing his moment of glory already receding into history.

Aaron is not unlike us when he seeks perfection. We all want some aspect of our lives to be perfect. Some of us have simpler expectations than others, but we all seek perfection or the ideal in some way. It might be finding the perfect vacation or bowling a perfect 300 game. It might be getting a maximum evaluation report at work or achieving all A's in school. It might even be being the perfect member in church, always tithing and volunteering above and beyond the call.

The reality is that we can never know more than a fleeting glance of perfection in our lives. Our moments of attaining the ideal are few and temporary. It's not for lack of trying that we fail to be consistently perfect. Rather it is because we live in a fallen, imperfect world, and await a fully redeemed state in which there will be no struggle with sin.

God is consistently perfect because He is the Author of perfection, of purity, of truth. He can be or do nothing less, because that is His nature. We, on the other hand, are His creations, limited in ability and further limited by our capacity to choose willingly between God's desires and our own desires, between good and evil, between eternity with God and eternity with Satan.

If we want to know God's will for our lives, we must understand His perfection and how it affects our relationship with Him. We must know that God is perfect and that He has established a standard to which we must conform if we are to know His will. When we know this part of His character, we can better understand how He will speak to us about how our lives may be fulfilled to glorify Him and how we may enjoy Him.

GOD IS HOLY

The God who possesses all power is also holy. What does it mean to be "holy"? It means to be "set apart." There is "no one holy like the Lord" (1 Samuel 2:2). When you pursue His will, you can know that it is pure and not tainted with evil. God's will for you is what is good and right and pure. God is so totally devoted to what is good that He has a perfect hatred for what is evil.

There is no debate in heaven about the truth of God's holiness. In fact at this moment the angels are around His throne singing, "Holy, Holy, Holy" (Isaiah 6:3). The debate is on earth, and it is God's will to communicate to man the truth of His holiness. One of the purposes of the great detailed account God has recorded in His Word of the building of the tabernacle and the various kinds of sacrifices is to impress us that God can be approached only in the way He has provided.

God's will is for you to understand and communicate His holiness. One proof that you are beginning to understand this attribute is humility. It is with the contrite and lowly that the Holy One dwells (Isaiah 57:15). Humility comes from understanding that we have no standing before God on our own. If all we ever did wrong was to think one impure thought, God would be totally just in sentencing us to hell forever.

A second proof that one is beginning to understand God's holiness is confidence in and gratefulness for Christ. As you seek God's will, you need two "new" legs on which to stand. One is the leg of humility that realizes you justly deserve His condemnation. The other leg is a great confidence in Jesus that enables you to come boldly to the throne of grace. One without the other would result in either pride or despair.

A third proof that you and I are beginning to know that God is holy is in our response to sin in our life. The response of confessing and forsaking our sin is contrasted in Proverbs 28:13 with covering it up. When I first moved to the Chicago area, I lived in the same apartment complex as Dr. Stephen Olford. I deeply appreciated his input into my life, and I do not think I will ever forget his words, "Be as sensitive to sin in your life as the pupil of your eye is to foreign matter."

A fourth proof is an attitude of complete trust in God's providential ways. Many things in life are hard to understand as we ponder, "Why did God let this happen?" The truth of God's holiness can enable us to say, "Lord, I don't understand why, but I know You are holy, and there is no taint of evil in You." The truth of God's holiness is a place of trust. As one person wisely said, "We can't always trace the hand of God, but we can always trust the heart of God." We can trust His heart because we know He is holy.

A fifth proof that we are coming to the knowledge of God's holiness is a joyful surrender of our lives to God. One of the reasons that Jesus came and shed His blood for us was to enable us to present our lives to Him. We are encouraged to present the totality of our lives to God that they can be used for His holy purposes.

> *Therefore I urge you, brethren, by the mercies of God, to present your bodies a living and holy sacrifice, acceptable to God, which is your spiritual service of worship. And do not be conformed to this world, but be transformed by the renewing of your mind, so that you may prove what the will of God is, that which is good and acceptable and perfect. (Romans 12:1–2)*

An eighty-five-year-old man was speaking on this theme one day in Dallas, and I will never forget his testimony. He said he had read Romans 12:1–2 as a seventeen-year-old boy and had been struck by it. He began to ask other Christians to explain it to him, but he received very little help. One day he was instructed to go to his room, get on his knees, put his finger on these verses, and tell God that he wanted to do it. He told how God illuminated to him that he was to surrender all parts of his body—his mind, imagination, eyes, ears, hands, feet, and so forth to God. He also related how that transaction with God almost seventy years before had made countless decisions for him and saved him from great harm.

I recall hearing Dr. Charles Stanley speak many years ago on "The Dedicated Life." His message was the inspiration for this prayer that I have shared with many people:

> *"Based on a right view of You and all that You have done for me in Christ, I joyfully make a definite commitment that I recognize Your ownership of my life. I yield every part of my life and all my possessions and relationships for Your possessions and control from this moment forth and forever. I am available for whatever You want, wherever You want it, and however You want it as long as I live. All my decisions will be based on this. I trust You and You alone to maintain this commitment.*
>
> *"For Your glory and my eternal benefit. Amen."*

GOD IS RIGHTEOUS

"When my enemies turn back, they stumble and perish before You. For You have maintained my just cause; You have sat on the throne judging righteously" (Psalm 9:3–4).

The desire to do God's will is a "just cause." There is no better cause than what we have just talked about—to be a vessel of God's love to the world. As a righteous God, He can be trusted to ultimately allow what is right to triumph.

There are four primary uses of the term *righteousness* in the Bible:

1. It refers to God's character as the moral governor of the universe (John 17:25).
2. It refers to the standard that God requires for one to be accepted by Him (Romans 3:10).
3. It refers to the standards by which Christians are to live (2 Timothy 2:22).
4. It refers to the gift of righteousness that God gives to all who trust Christ (Romans 5:17).

How do these truths help us in pursuing God's will? They let us know that the most basic aspect of God's will is to receive His gift of righteousness and come to know His acceptance as our righteous heavenly Father. They also tell us to pursue righteousness, which is a life that conforms to God's kind ways.

Because He is righteous He has promised to vindicate His people when they suffer for doing what is right. I was talking to a missionary one night who was agonizing over the vicious, unfair opposition that he was receiving from fellow missionaries. What keeps one going in such cases? What aids us in not seeking to vindicate ourselves and take our own revenge? It is trusting in God's righteousness. "Truthful lips will be established forever, but a lying tongue is only for a moment" (Proverbs 12:19). "Like a sparrow in its flitting, like a swallow in its flying, so a curse without cause does not alight" (Proverbs 26:2).

For this reason we can be encouraged to follow the amazing admonition of Peter—"Not returning evil for evil or insult for insult, but giving a blessing instead; for you were called for the very purpose that you might inherit a blessing" (1 Peter 3:9).

Such was the example of Christ (1 Peter 2:21–23) and of the apostle Paul (2 Timothy 4:14). As we give in to anger we can easily be diverted from doing the will of God. Do you think that God is indifferent to your hurt? He is not. It is only that God does not want you to have to bear the burden of dishing out justice. Tell God about your pain and ask Him to put His healing touch upon it. Commit the one who hurt you into the hands of God and be available to be a blessing to that person. This would be an impossible assignment apart from the supernatural enablement of God.

God can also be trusted to graciously reward you for every work of faith you do that is motivated by love, as these Scripture passages indicate:

> *"One who is gracious to a poor man lends to the Lord, and He will repay him for his good deed." (Proverbs 19:17)*

"And everyone who has left houses or brothers or sisters or father or mother or children or farms for My name's sake, will receive many times as much, and will inherit eternal life." (Matthew 19:29)

"For whoever gives you a cup of water to drink because of your name as followers of Christ, truly I say to you, he will not lose his reward." (Mark 9:41)

"Do not be deceived, God is not mocked; for whatever a man sows, this he will also reap. For the one who sows to his own flesh will from the flesh reap corruption, but the one who sows to the Spirit will from the Spirit reap eternal life. Let us not lose heart in doing good, for in due time we will reap if we do not grow weary." (Galatians 6:7–9)

"For God is not unjust so as to forget your work and the love which you have shown toward His name, in having ministered and in still ministering to the saints." (Hebrews 6:10)

You will probably be tempted to lose heart in your pursuit of doing the will of God. An amazing passage in Isaiah prophetically speaks of Christ and reveals the temptation to lose heart: "He said to Me, 'You are My Servant, Israel, in Whom I will show My glory.' But I said, 'I have toiled in vain, I have spent My strength for nothing and vanity; yet surely the justice due to Me is with the Lord, and My reward with My God'" (Isaiah

49:3–4). Dr. Raymond Edmond, past president of Wheaton College, often encouraged people by telling them it was too soon to quit.

I remember hearing the oft-told story of a missionary who returned home from many years of sacrificial service. At the same time, former President Roosevelt was coming back from a hunting trip in Africa. As President Roosevelt returned, music bands were there to greet him and there was a big to-do over his returning. The longer the missionary observed this, the more bitter he was tempted to get. He turned to his wife and said, "How come nobody is here to greet us when we arrive home?" She wisely replied, "We haven't come home yet." God meets our needs here, but payday is in the future and God is not unjust so as to forget your labor—not even a cup of cold water given in His name. "Nothing is lost that is done for the Lord, let it be ever so small, the smile of the Savior approves of the deed as though it were the greatest of all."—Author Unknown

GOD IS FAITHFUL AND TRUE

George Mueller was burdened to encourage people to experience the faithfulness of God. He founded an orphanage not only because he cared about the needy children but because he wanted God's people to see that He is faithful and will answer prayer. He saw older people living in fear of whether they would be forsaken by God. He saw people operating unethically in their careers because they feared that they could not compete if they lived honestly in the business world. To honor God's faithfulness was his objective in starting an orphanage and making his needs known only to God. In his lifetime he recorded more than fifty thousand answers to prayer, and many of these are found in the book *Answers to Prayer*.[1]

It is God's will to use your life to show the world that God is faithful. While all of life is a time to lean on God's faithfulness, Scripture highlights the following specific times.

1. *At the beginning of each day.*

Lamentations 3:22–23 is probably the best-known Old Testament verse on the faithfulness of God. It says, "The Lord's lovingkindnesses indeed never cease, for His compassions never fail. They are new every morning; great is Your faithfulness." There is something special about the beginning of a day. Someone has wisely said, "Many a strong man gets pinned by the sheets every morning." Getting out of bed is more than just a physical phenomenon. The bed can feel so cozy and secure because of a conscious or an unconscious thought about something we do not want to face that day. This is why God says to step out of bed depending on His faithfulness!

2. *During trials and temptations.*

"No temptation has overtaken you but such as is common to man; and God is faithful, who will not allow you to be tempted beyond what you are able, but with the temptation will provide the way of escape also, so that you will be able to endure it" (1 Corinthians 10:13). "But the Lord is faithful, and He will strengthen and protect you from the evil one" (2 Thessalonians 3:3). As long as we are in this body we will be tempted. We can look to a faithful God to prepare us for temptations, and sometimes this means not making provisions for fleshly desires (Romans 13:14).

A generous family gave a godly friend of mine free room and board while he was doing his seminary work. His room had access to cable television. On occasion he found himself looking at things that would defile him. It happened on numerous occasions, and after a lengthy struggle he graciously and gratefully moved out. He did not try to put any blame on anybody else, but he knew for him that this was making provisions for the flesh. This area may not be your problem, but you may have a struggle in another area. Leaning on God's faithfulness means considering the possibility of temptation before it comes as well as trusting God in the temptation itself.

A pastor on the West Coast was leading a number of people to Christ from a variety of difficult backgrounds. He told them that after coming to Christ they would be tempted to go back to some of their wrong choices. He instructed them to think ahead of a prayer that they would pray every time they were tempted in this problem area. He said, "Let it be a prayer that would damage Satan's kingdom if God were to answer it." This proved to be a great help. You also can apply it to any persistent temptation in your life. It is one way of leaning on God's faithfulness as you encounter temptation.

3. *When we suffer for doing right.*

"Therefore, those also who suffer according to the will of God shall entrust their souls to a faithful Creator in doing what is right" (1 Peter 4:19). As we suffer we can seek God to see if our sin is the cause of the suffering. I can suffer for righteousness, but I can also bring suffering upon my life by my own sinful attitude and actions. When our consciences are clear, we need to put the suffering in perspective and ask God what good He desires to come out of it (Romans 8:18; 2 Corinthians 1:3–11). Many significant ministries have occurred during times of great trial. *Pilgrim's Progress* and many of Paul's epistles were written from prison.

4. *When we are in need of cleansing.*

"If we confess our sins, He is faithful and righteous to forgive us our sins and to cleanse us from all unrighteousness" (1 John 1:9). God is not only faithful to lovingly convict us but also to lovingly cleanse us.

5. *When we think about the future.*

"Now may the God of peace Himself sanctify you entirely; and may your spirit and soul and body be preserved complete, without blame at the coming of our Lord Jesus Christ. Faithful is He who calls you, and He also will bring it to pass" (1 Thessalonians 5:23–24).

These verses speak of our ultimate future. Christ wisely told us not to be anxious for tomorrow. God's will can only be lived one day at a time.

As you focus on God's faithfulness and truthfulness, you will be saved from despair. In your faithlessness He remains faithful (2 Timothy 2:13), and as you repent of your sin, He will faithfully cleanse you (1 John 1:9). You will also become like the one upon whom you concentrate. If you are bitter at another person, you tend to become like that person. If you focus on God's glorious character, He will do a transforming work in your life (2 Corinthians 3:18). God desires to transform you into a faithful and true person. What does the Scripture say about this character quality?

- Faithfulness will give you favor with God and man (Proverbs 3:3–4).
- Faithfulness is an extremely rare quality (Proverbs 20:6).
- Faithfulness begins with the little areas of life (Luke 16:10).
- Faithfulness is a work of God's Spirit in us (Galatians 5:22–23).

A young businessman came to me one day and asked me about God's standard of truthfulness. He said that his boss did not expect him to be honest and honesty could hinder his business pursuits. We went to the book of Proverbs and discussed these verses.

"A worthless person, a wicked man, is the one who walks with a perverse mouth." (Proverbs 6:12)

"There are six things which the Lord hates, yes, seven which are an abomination to Him: haughty eyes, a lying tongue . . ." (Proverbs 6:16)

"Truthful lips will be established forever, but a lying tongue is only for a moment." (Proverbs 12:19)

"Lying lips are an abomination to the Lord, but those who deal faithfully are His delight." (Proverbs 12:22)

"A false witness will not go unpunished, and he who tells lies will not escape." (Proverbs 19:5)

"The acquisition of treasures by a lying tongue is a fleeting vapor, the pursuit of death." (Proverbs 21:6)

His heart was tender and persuaded. He walked away desiring to be a man of truth. May God give each of us the grace to be a man or woman of truth. This is clearly God's will for us.

NOTE

1. George Mueller, *Answers to Prayer* (Chicago: Moody, n.d.).

◆

Chapter Eight

The Passion
of God

Love is a term that is freely used in today's culture. Sometimes it refers to compassion for less fortunate people, like the elderly or the homeless. Sometimes it refers to care within a family for one another. Other times, it has a strictly sensual connotation that is not always accompanied by any genuine feelings of warmth.

Perhaps the most overused example hearkens back to our own desire for satisfaction, for fulfillment, from whatever source it may come. We've all heard or used expressions like "I'd love to own a car like that," or "I love pepperoni pizza with green peppers," or "Downhill skiing is my true love." Answering the call of love is our most fundamental need. God designed us to need and experience love. He, the all-wise Creator and loving Lord, wasn't making any mistakes when He fashioned our bodies and souls this way.

But in the same way that we were made to receive love, we were also designed to express love. How do we express love? We might send cards and presents to family members on their birthdays. We love our spouses, having perhaps gone through an elaborate courtship to prove it. We might also donate generously to the more needy in our culture or in distant lands.

Let's look at the two aspects of love, receiving and expressing. Do we have any problem receiving love? Sometimes, but usually not, especially when some inner need is fulfilled. Do we have problems expressing love? If you are honest with yourself, you will probably answer yes. And there's a good reason for that.

Love, in its truest form, is sacrificial. That means when you care about someone enough, you will give up something to fulfill the needs of that other party. It might be time, money, energy, emotion, or perhaps even your life. For people who are naturally self-absorbed, sacrificing for others doesn't come readily, or at least as readily as receiving love does.

As with power and knowledge, God is the Author and Creator of love. His sacrificial love is evident to us every day just in our own existence. God went to the trouble to create you in all your own individualized complexity, to give you life and a unique purpose designed just for you in His created world. He didn't do it because He was bored. He did it because He dearly loves His children. And He nurtures us, picking us up after we stumble, ethically and spiritually, yearning that we will dedicate our lives to acknowledging and glorifying Him.

Ever wonder how things would be if you were king (or God)? Would ruthless dictators still be in power? I'm guessing that you, given the chance to serve as ultimate arbiter of justice in the world, would tell them that they have blown it and immediately dish out justice. No trial or opportunity to confess for them.

Or what about the person who lied to you and broke a promise? Even worse is the person who falsely accused you and the employer who treated you unfairly. What is your response to the one who cheated you financially or the loved one who rejected you? This kind of pain requires a love beyond our own resources.

If God took each of our own transgressions against His will with the same limited capacity for sacrificial love that we demonstrate, most of us wouldn't get out of the starting gate of life, and the rest wouldn't last long afterward. We don't have to be evil dictators to break God's heart. We can simply fail to give our children the daily dose of love and encouragement they need, forget to show compassion to a hurting coworker because we're too busy, or be negligent in our giving to God because we really need that new set of golf clubs.

Fortunately, our God looks at the bigger picture, and with an idea toward redeeming us to Him. He put His Son here on earth in human form to exercise unconditional love toward us, that we might be restored to His grace through the atoning sacrifice of Jesus Christ's death on the cross. We can see this more fully as we examine the aspects that represent this incredible love.

GOD IS LOVE

But Zion said, "The Lord has forsaken me, and the Lord has forgotten me."

"Can a woman forget her nursing child and have no compassion on the son of her womb? Even these may forget, but I will not forget you. Behold, I have inscribed you on the palms of My hands; your walls are continually before Me." (Isaiah 49:14–16)

In describing God's love for His people, Isaiah likens it to the love of a mother for her nursing child and then declares it to be much greater and more dependable. You can never overemphasize God's love. It is an infinite love, and God can love you as if you were the only person in the world (cf. Galatians 2:20). He can give you His complete attention and not be inattentive to anyone else. His love is also holy, and He will discipline you when necessary to restore you to Himself (Hebrews 12:5–6).

Reading 1 Corinthians 13:1–3 one comes to the conclusion that whatever love is, it is the most important thing in God's economy. As I pondered this obvious truth one year, I also came to the idea that if "we love, because He first loved us" (1 John 4:19) there is one vital command for me. I must grow in the understanding of His love for me so that I can better respond in loving Him and others.

I went into one new year with the prayer request, "Lord, overwhelm me with Your love." As I trusted God with this petition, familiar passages began to open up like never before. Meditating on Romans 5:8–11, I examined the descriptions of whom it is God loves— the helpless, ungodly, sinners, and His enemies. Many times I have felt helpless, and I have praised Him for His love. If you have trusted Jesus, you are no longer His enemy, but His beloved child. You should not seek God's will in order to do something to earn His love. You should humble yourself before Him and let Him love you in a way that wins your heart to Him.

How do you know if you are beginning to be overwhelmed with His love? One evidence is when you sense that God loves you in a way that no one else ever will or can. He is better than the best of men (Romans 5:7–8). In fact as I read the Scripture's command for me to love, I begin to see how it is that God has first loved me that way. For example as I would read "A friend loves at all times," I thanked God that He loves me at all times. That is also the reassurance I need to be this kind of friend (Proverbs 17:17). As God encouraged me to forgive others rather than remind them of their failures, I praised Him that He does not rub my past shortcomings in my face (Proverbs 17:9).

God loves you, and while you cannot merit or earn His love, you can put yourself in a position to enjoy it. Parents can love their rebellious child just as much as their submissive child, but the latter will experience more of that love. As we live under Christ's loving control, we can understand and experience the various dimensions of God's love according to Ephesians 3:14–19.

Although it is clearly God's command to love Him supremely (Matthew 22:37–39), we need to beware of other competing loves:

Love for world—1 John 2:15
Love for money—1 Timothy 6:10
Love for pleasure—2 Timothy 3:4
Love for self—2 Timothy 3:2

God wants us to know His love in a way that we respond in loving Him supremely and seeking to be a vessel of love for others. God's will for you is the way in which you can best know God's love and respond to it by loving Him and others supremely.

The reference to Philippians 1:9–11 is engraved on the band of Penny's and my wedding rings. As you do God's will, continue to lay this prayer before His throne day by day:

And this I pray, that your love [for God and others] may abound still more and more in real knowledge and all discernment, so that you may approve the things that are excellent, in order to be sincere and blameless until the day of Christ; having been filled with the fruit of righteousness which comes through Jesus Christ, to the glory and praise of God.

GOD IS MERCIFUL

God is merciful in that He not only feels for us in our misery and distress but He sends compassionate help. As we seek God's will, we must admit that we are not capable in ourselves to discern His will (Jeremiah 10:23) and that we have enemies who are too strong for us. We are to rely on His help. It is God's will for you to experience His salvation (Ephesians 2:4–5) and His merciful plan of service for you. Despite the fact that Paul had actively opposed Christ and killed Christians, God mercifully saved him and, in his words, put him "into service" (1 Timothy 1:12–13). Even after being placed into service, he said he would have given up and lost heart were it not for God's mercy and help (2 Corinthians 4:1). Even his own transformed character is attributed to God's mercy (1 Corinthians 7:25) and His comfort in trials (2 Corinthians 1:3–5).

The implications should be obvious. God also has a merciful plan for you in spite of your past sin. I will never forget the statement that I heard as a college student, "Any time a person is surrendered to God, He has a special plan for his life." In fact, His mercy is used as the motivation to present our bodies to Him (Romans 12:1–2). As John Calvin said, "Men will never worship God with a sincere heart and be roused to fear and obey Him with sufficient zeal until they properly understand how much indebted they are to His mercy."

Do you have any fear of pursuing the will of God?

After I had surrendered my life to the Lord as a college student, I became involved with a Christian campus organization. We would go to some small towns in Alabama to conduct Christian living seminars on Friday night and Saturday and then speak in churches on Sunday. I knew very little, and often all I could say was my testimony. After I had spoken to an adult Sunday school class, a well-meaning lady came up to me and said, "Great suffering is ahead for you." Such a statement struck great fear in my heart. After that any time a person talked about trials, a cloud seemed to come over me. The Scripture that God used to remove that cloud was 2 Corinthians 1:5. This verse says that whatever we go through, God's merciful comfort will be there: "For just as the sufferings of Christ are ours in abundance, so also our comfort is abundant through Christ." It is not God's will for us to live in fear of what might happen. In fact, "Who is there to harm you if you prove zealous for what is good?" (1 Peter 3:13). God is merciful, and we are to imitate His mercy to others by giving to those in need and offering mercy to others (Luke 6:36–38).

GOD IS GRACIOUS

Apart from God's grace, where would you and I be today? We would be in a place of eternal torment and misery that the Bible calls hell. Anything we ever receive in life other than His judgment is due to God's grace. Part of the problem in seeking God's will is all of the expectations we bring to the table. We think, *I deserve a healthy body, a nice house, healthy and intelligent children, and whatever else I want.* There is nothing necessarily wrong with any of these desires. However, not only does this thinking destroy a grateful spirit, but it also sets us up to be bitter.

> "I can be grateful when God's will includes things above my expectations."
>
> ▲
>
> *(expectations line)* "I deserve this."
> _____
>
> ▼
>
> "I can be bitter when God's will doesn't meet my expectations."

God in His grace has given us His salvation. In His grace believers are the children of a heavenly King. He will provide all we need to do His will, for we stand in His favor (Romans 5:2)! We can know God's full acceptance. This may not be a new thought, but the question is not have we heard it, but are we resting in this truth. If we never have times of spontaneously praising God for His all-embracing acceptance, the evidence is that we are not resting in it. If our prayers are not characterized by complete honesty and intimacy, we are not resting in it. You will only be truly honest and intimate with one who you know graciously loves and accepts you. It is God's will for us to rest in this grace and allow it to overflow in love and forgiveness to others.

God's grace can also enable you to do God's will.

The apostle Paul wrote, "But by the grace of God I am what I am, and His grace toward me did not prove vain; but I labored even more than all of them, yet not I, but the grace of God with me" (1 Corinthians 15:10). His grace in this verse speaks of His motivation and enabling to do God's will. Good deeds done in the energy of the flesh will lose their ability to stimulate you. Only God's grace can keep you going. You can ask Paul when you get to heaven, "Did you feel like being godly every day? Did you even feel like getting up every day?" I am sure he will tell you, "No. It was only my dependence on God's grace that kept me going."

We need God's grace for all that we do, and for that reason 2 Corinthians 8 speaks even of the grace of giving. It has been said that the last part of a man's body to get sanctified is his hip pocket. As a high school student, I occasionally put a dollar in the offering plate, and a friend would punch me and say, "That is one less dollar you have to buy the car you're saving for." The sad thing is that is how I thought about it too. After college and before seminary God prompted me to give away my summer salary. Because this was so different from my past action, no one could doubt that it was a result of God's gracious motivation and enabling and not my own generosity.

This reminds me of a story that Billy Graham told when he went to encourage a group of missionaries who had suffered the loss of all their belongings due to a political change in the country they were serving. He told them of a billionaire who was speaking to a church and telling how God had blessed him. The wealthy man said that it all started many years ago when he had a dollar in one hand and a quarter in the other as the offering plate was being passed. This was all the money he had. He related the struggle in his own soul. "Will it be the dollar, or will it be the quarter that I give?" He said that when the offering plate came to him, "I just gave it all, and that is why the Lord has so blessed me." As he finished, a little lady in the back said, "I dare him to do it again!"

It is one thing for us to talk of the grace of God in the distant past, but the question is what are we doing today in response to the Lord's gracious enabling. Billy Graham told the missionaries that when they came to the mission field, they had given up everything and God was encouraging them to do it again.

When Corrie ten Boom went back to Germany to speak on forgiveness to a guilt-laden people, her former prison guard came up to her after her talk. She said as he stretched out his hand to her, anger boiled up inside of her with the thought of how her sister had been so cruelly beaten by this particular guard. She prayed, "O God, please help me" and before she knew what she was doing she had her hand in his and was saying, "I forgive you." God's grace is the enabling we need to do His will.

GOD IS GOOD

We stated earlier that the basic strategy of Satan is

to distort our understanding of God. He seeks to attack God's goodness in order to make a person feel that obeying God will shortchange his or her life. God is good and His ways are always good. He says that if we seek the primary thing we will get the secondary things. Look at these verses that amplify this message.

"But seek first His kingdom and His righteousness, and all these things will be added to you." (Matthew 6:33) Our responsibility is to seek His rule, and His responsibility is to provide for our needs.

Psalm 84:11 says, "For the Lord God is a sun and shield; the Lord gives grace and glory; no good thing does He withhold from those who walk uprightly." Our responsibility is to walk uprightly, and His responsibility is to give us the good things.

Psalm 37:4 instructs us, "Delight yourself in the Lord; and He will give you the desires of your heart." Our responsibility is to delight in God, and His responsibility is to give us the desires of our hearts.

John Wesley is often quoted with the words, "Don't seek for a ministry, but anticipate the fruit of a disciplined life." As we respond to the character of God, the experience of God's will is the overflow of this relationship. Knowing God's will is a result of knowing God.

God's good gifts do sometimes come in disguised

packages. Anything in your life that encourages you to seek God is good from God's perspective. The continual temptation to fear is to encourage you to seek God. The psalmist said, "I sought the Lord, and He answered me, and delivered me from all my fears" (Psalm 34:4). God is encouraging you to seek God in order that He can spiritually prosper you. Second Chronicles 26:5 says of the ancient king Uzziah, "As long as he sought the Lord, God prospered him." The good gift of trials enables you to know God's comfort and enrich your soul. A Puritan writer said that if someone threw a bag of gold at you and it hit you and temporarily knocked you out, you would not attack the person when you woke up and discovered the bag of gold. Trials do temporarily knock you out, but they also enrich your life.

It is not often you will be in a prayer meeting and hear someone praying for the good gift of loneliness. However, if your loneliness encourages you to cultivate the companionship of Jesus, it is a good gift. God has placed you in a spiritual battle. Sometimes it is very intense and, if you are like me, there are days when your greatest goal is surviving the day. This battle enables us to see the preciousness of Jesus and to see also that He is not just nice but absolutely necessary.

As you seek His will, realize that God is good and yearns to bless you. I think I used to look at God through the glasses of my guilty conscience rather than through Christ. The question is not whether you or I deserve His blessing, for we do not, but, rather, will we humble ourselves before God and receive the spiritual blessings that Jesus shed His blood to give us. Perhaps the following prayer represents the desire of your heart. If so, pray it in faith to your heavenly Father: "Do whatever You need to do inside me to fully illuminate my total being to see Your goodness in a way that wins my very heart to You."

NOTE: To reflect on what we have explored so far, go to the personal journal on page 194.

Knowing
God's Desire
for You

Chapter Nine

How God Speaks to Us in Everyday Life

1 f you had to identify the principal source of anxiety of people who debate the existence of God, it would probably be the issue of communication. No one gets phone calls or e-mails from God. He doesn't appear to us, even in some spectral form, to tell us His desire for us.

Hollywood produces movies and television shows that have God appearing in some more tangible form so that people can dialogue with Him. However we should not look to Hollywood to get our understanding of God. Authors have produced serious books in recent years, claiming to have had numerous intimate conversations with the Almighty. Again the message of these books is dubious at best and inconsistent with the God of the

Bible. As we learned in the previous chapters covering God's attributes, if God is anything, He is consistent in His character. He cannot be or do things that are not in His divine nature, despite the fact that He is all-knowing and all-powerful. God sent His Son, Jesus Christ, to us in human form so that He could dialogue with us and tell us of the Creator's will for His people.

God is a God who communicates to us. It would be very difficult to have a relationship with someone who never spoke. We will look at four ways in which God speaks to His people.

1. God speaks through Scripture.
2. God speaks through the prompting of His Spirit.
3. God speaks through people.
4. God speaks through circumstances.

Number 1 is the primary way and numbers 2 through 4 are the secondary ways. The secondary ways must always be evaluated under the authority of the Scriptures.

GOD SPEAKS THROUGH SCRIPTURE

"Your word is a lamp to my feet and a light to my path" (Psalm 119:105). "All Scripture is inspired by God and profitable for teaching, for reproof, for correction, for training in righteousness; so that the man of God may be adequate, equipped for every good work" (2 Timothy 3:16–17).

God has clearly laid out principles for us to follow in His Word to do His will. We can follow the general principles; the particulars may be left for us to discern. For example God explicitly says that it is His will for people to be saved from His eternal wrath and to come to the knowledge of the truth (1 Timothy 2:4; 2 Peter 3:9). This general principle should be considered as we ask questions like these:

- How does God desire to use me as an instrument of this salvation?
- Would I be a better instrument if I were single or married?
- How does this affect my choice of vocation?
- How does this affect where God wants me to live?
- How does this affect my purchases?

Many other clear scriptural principles reveal His will. For example:

- It is God's will for you to live in moral purity and to be set apart for Him (1 Thessalonians 4:3).
- It is God's will that you rejoice always, pray without ceasing, and give thanks in everything (1 Thessalonians 5:16–18).
- It is God's will for you to submit to the authorities of your life (Romans 13:1).

You could probably add many other clear commands of Scripture to this list.

Evaluating Our Actions by Scripture

Numerous scriptural principles can aid you in determining whether something is right for you or not. The primary one is simple and obvious, but sometimes overlooked: *Do the Scriptures forbid it?* Believers have been known to justify clear violations of Scripture with excuses ranging from "The Holy Spirit told me it's OK" to "I deserve it, and lots of people my age do it."

Another question to ask is, *Will it cause me to be tempted to sin* (Romans 13:14)? A given action might not be intrinsically right or wrong, but it might entice your sinful tendencies and thus be wrong for you. A similar question to ask is this: *Is it an "encumbrance" or something that hinders my Christian life* (Hebrews 12:1)? A relationship, a possession, or even a hobby may not be wrong in itself but can be a hindrance to God's call on your life.

What you are considering might be acceptable under the previous guidelines. If so, you may want to ask, *Is it approving the things that are excellent, and will it profit me spiritually?* In other words, is it the best choice I could make, or is it only acceptable?

When the choice is something you really enjoy doing, sometimes it is necessary to ask, *Does it tend to control me* (1 Corinthians 6:12)? There is a fine line between deeply enjoying something and being controlled by it. There is not necessarily anything wrong with enjoying your favorite sports team, but whether they win or lose should not dictate whether or not you can have a good day. I remember listening to my college football team play one night when there were six lead changes. My emotions were up, then down, up, then down, and then up! They won, but before the end of the game, I realized that my focus needed to be on what does not change and not on the changeable. Spouses may need to ask themselves whether an activity is taking too much time away from the family or the spouse.

Some issues might be perfectly acceptable to our own conscience but troublesome to others. So another relevant question is, *Is it a stumbling stone* (Romans 14; 1 Corinthians 8)? We should not do anything that would encourage another to go against his conscience. Our own entertainment or our "freedom in Christ" is not worth harm to a brother or sister in Christ.

Relevant especially to our interaction with unbelievers is another query: *Does it give an unnecessary offense to others* (1 Corinthians 9:19–21; 10:32; Colossians 4:5)? The Gospel is an offense, but we are not to be one ourselves unnecessarily.

And finally, does it live up to our high calling to be imitators of Christ? *Does it draw attention to God's character* (1 Corinthians 10:31)? And, *Can I do it in faith (Romans 14:14, 22–23) and love* (1 Corinthians 13:1–3)?

Following God's Guidance in Scripture

We will undoubtedly get off track if we fail to follow the clear guidance that God has already given. We can spend so much time debating particular gray areas that we forget more obvious, clear areas of obedience. We know that it is God's will for us to love Him today with all of our being and to be an instrument of love to others (Matthew 22:37–39). God usually guides us one step at a time; His guidance is given within the framework of present obedience.

God gave Balaam a clear word not to go with the elders of Moab and not to curse God's people (Numbers 22:12). Balaam proceeded to ask God again on the matter that He had already made very clear and finally got permission (Numbers 22:19–20). Although God gave permission for him to go, He was not pleased (Numbers 22:22). If we insist on having our own way though it is against God's revealed will, we may get it and regret that we did (Psalm 106:13–15).

Meditating on Scripture

In order to listen to God through Scripture you need to meditate on it. There is a continual battle between the worldly and the divine for the control of our minds. Only the continual renewal of our minds through meditation will lead us to experience God's good, acceptable, and perfect will (Romans 12:2). Meditation on Scripture is a discipline that God promises to bless. Listen to the testimony of God's Word.

For on the first of the first month he began to go up from Babylon; and on the first of the fifth month he came to Jerusalem, **because the good hand of his God was upon him. For Ezra had set his heart** to study the law of the Lord and to practice it, and to teach His statutes and ordinances in Israel. (Ezra 7:9–10)

This book of the law shall not depart from your mouth, but you **shall meditate on it day and night,** so that you may be careful to do according to all that is written in it; for then you will make your way **prosperous,** and then you will have **success.** Have I not commanded you? Be strong and courageous! Do not tremble or be dismayed, for the Lord you God is with you wherever you go. (Joshua 1:8–9)

How blessed is the man who does not walk in the counsel of the wicked, nor stand in the path of sinners, nor sit in the seat of scoffers! But his delight is in the law of the Lord, and in His law he **meditates day and night.** And he will be like a tree firmly planted by streams of water, which yields its fruit in its season and its leaf does not wither; and in whatever he does, he **prospers.** (Psalm 1:1–3)

But one who looks intently at the perfect law, the law of liberty, and abides by it, not having become a forgetful hearer but an effectual doer, this man will be **blessed** in what he does. (James 1:25)

The Bible is the only book whose Author is always present when one reads it. Meditation is simply talking to God about His Word with the goal of your life coming into agreement with it. It is God's will to make this the priority of your life. George Mueller is probably best known as a man of faith. He trusted God to provide for his needs as he cared for hundreds of orphans. In the biography *George Mueller of Bristol,* A. T. Pierson relates how God convicted Mueller of his greater devotion to Christian books than to the Bible. He responded to this conviction, and his biographer reports that in the ninety-second year of his life, for every page he read in other books, he read proportionately ten pages of the Scripture. The result was a life of amazing fruitfulness. Perhaps George Mueller should be known more as a man who delighted in God and in His Word than in his faith in God to provide for orphans. When I was in seminary, a chapel speaker quoted an older man who at the end of his life held up his Bible as he was speaking to a group of men and said, "Men, I wish I had read this book more and other books less!"

Why not trust God to give you a plan to study, memorize, and meditate on Scripture? Ask God to give you somebody to do it with as an encouragement. I find it helpful to carry around 3 x 5 cards with the passage that I am studying and memorizing in order to use the spare moments of the day to meditate on it. I know there is a battle in my mind, and *I always need something to refresh my mind for the next skirmish.*

On an annual retreat that our family takes with two other families, I sensed the battle for my mind in a way I never previously had. I was preaching a series on anger at a church, and I believe that God was giving some helpful principles. This particular weekend I arrived at the conclusion that in order to practice these principles, the discipline of continual meditation on Scripture is essential. That is the only way to redirect the wrong patterns to process frustration we have in our thinking.

That weekend, one of the other fathers told how he grieved over the sense that his marriage had seemed to plateau spiritually. He had a burden for spiritual progress in his marriage, but the things that he desired to take place simply were not happening. One day after hearing a message on Scripture meditation, he went to his wife and said, "Would you please forgive me for the lack of spiritual progress in our relationship?" He took responsibility for the lack of progress and quit blaming her. He then began to do what he had been exhorted to do in the message he had heard. The principle of John 17:19 had been given. Jesus set Himself apart in order that His disciples might be set apart in faith. The husband was encouraged to take all his energy and devotion to setting his life apart through meditation in Scripture. When he wanted something to happen in his wife's life, he began meditating on Scripture in that area and asked God to do it in him. As he began to do that, he saw things happen in the next six months that he had longed to take place. His wife did not know what he was doing, but she certainly knew the benefits! The energy that he had been using to change his wife was redirected into meditating on Scripture, which God used to help him truly love his wife!

The night after I heard this testimony, I went to bed meditating on Psalm 144:1–2. My six-year-old son vomited in the night; for the rest of the night every time he moved, I jumped to get a trash can. I did not sleep at all. That night was one of the worst of my life as I battled weariness and spiritual discouragement. Since I could not sleep and felt the need to talk with God, I got up and sought the Lord in prayer, but I still felt discouraged. I turned to the Bible and repeatedly read Psalm 144:1–2. Then I read Psalm 145 and began to say Psalm 145:1–2 to the Lord and also Psalm 145:14, "The Lord sustains all who fall and raises up all who are bowed down."

The next morning I went to get my son some cola to drink, and I met a friend. He was going to give a testimony that day at church, and I told him how Psalm 145:14 had given me hope the night before. It seemed to be exactly what he needed to hear. As we seek the Lord and meditate on His Word, it does not take away all problems. However, He can spiritually prosper us in our trials and work through us in our weakness.

I began to study, memorize, and meditate on one passage after another. Some of them were Exodus 20, Matthew 5:1–12, John 15, Romans 6, Ephesians 6:10–20, Colossians 3, and 1 Thessalonians 4. I kept in mind that the goal in meditation is not just to gain new insight but to gain a greater intimacy with Christ. I cannot quote all of what I have memorized word for word. One can memorize a passage the second or third time through a little more easily, but the primary goal is to let the truth transform our lives.

God gave great initial encouragement by deepening the ministry I was having. In a period of a couple of weeks several individuals with whom I had been in regular contact began to tell me their deeper struggles. My youngest son at the time also called me at work and told me he had trusted Jesus! I rejoiced because he had been showing some resistance to the Lord. His salvation was a special answer to the prayers of his brother, who had gone to sleep in tears many a night praying for him.

Charles Spurgeon said, "Nobody ever outgrows Scripture; the Bible widens and deepens with our years." Ask God to give you an unquenchable thirst for it. It is the primary means by which God discloses His will and the standard by which any other means must be evaluated.

GOD SPEAKS THROUGH
THE PROMPTING OF HIS SPIRIT

This is not an easy one to write about because it can be so easily abused. I am not saying that every time you need to make a decision, God will give you a clear, sudden, and definite disclosure to your conscience by His Spirit apart from His Word. When one sees this as the sole (or even the primary) way to discern God's will, he or she will get into bondage and eventually come to discount the entire idea that God's will can be known. I believe that this is a secondary means that God uses to speak to us and that what we believe to be the Holy Spirit's nudging must be scrutinized by comparison with Scripture. This will ensure that it is in fact the Holy Spirit and not some subconscious whim.

Not every strong urge is a prompting from God. We can be tempted not only to desire but even to crave the wrong things (1 Corinthians 10:6). Our responsibility is to get to know the Shepherd, and then we will be able to discern His voice (John 10:4). Discernment is a fruit of the presentation of our lives to God (Romans 12:1–2). Jesus promised spiritual discernment to a person who is willing to do His will (John 7:17).

God can put ideas into your mind. Note how Nehemiah testified to the idea of God putting ideas into his mind (Nehemiah 2:12) and his heart (7:5). Although we do not depend on the Holy Spirit's direct leading for every decision of our lives, and although expecting it for every decision or overanalyzing events to discern God's leading can be abused, we need to be open to it and not discount it altogether.

God gave Caleb a vision for what He desired to do (Numbers 13:30). Dr. Bill Bright has told how God laid on his heart the vision for Campus Crusade for Christ while he was studying for a Greek exam. God put in the heart of David a desire to build a temple for the Lord, even though his son actually built it (2 Chronicles 6:7–9). God can also put restraints on our hearts, as we see in Acts 16:7.

Every genuine prompting of the Spirit will be in harmony with the balanced teaching of Scripture and will never contradict it, for the Spirit is called the Spirit of truth (John 15:26). The prompting of God's Holy Spirit is opposite to the flesh, which lusts against the Spirit (Galatians 5:17). These promptings are inward urges to do God's will, "for it is God who is at work in you, both to will and to work for His good pleasure" (Philippians 2:13). They are not to be divorced from the other means of God's communications. They come by the reading of the Bible and godly teaching and preaching as well as godly counsel.

GOD SPEAKS THROUGH PEOPLE

An unwillingness to take advice from others can get a person into great problems. A wise person is characterized as one who listens to counsel (Proverbs 12:15). One should especially be attentive to the counsel of the key people in one's life, such as parents and pastors. When I was considering doctoral studies, I wrote to a number of godly educators all across the nation as I pondered my next step. I also wrote to my mom, and the letter I got back from her was perhaps the greatest help.

Our parents know us, and even when they have a different spiritual frame of reference, they can give us insights. In fact it can be helpful to ask them to point out our blind spots or areas of weakness of which we may not be aware. It takes great maturity to truly absorb what they say about our blind spots, as well as to explain our personal convictions to our parents without a spirit of condemnation when theirs differ from ours.

Counsel can be used by God to enable us to think of the long-term consequences of a decision. If you plan to marry somebody based strictly on appearances, you need to realize that in twenty years the person's appearance may have changed greatly. We do not need to be paralyzed by thinking of the future impact of our decisions, but it does deserve consideration.

If one extreme is being unwilling to accept counsel, the other extreme is an insistence that someone else make all of your decisions for you. I admire a gentleman in Scripture named Apollos because of his courage to obey God and wait on His timing. The apostle Paul came to him and gave him great encouragement to go with a group of other believers to Corinth. He could have reasoned, "The apostle Paul has encouraged me to do this, so it must be God's will." However, he was preoccupied with obeying God and not man. I also admire Paul for his good word of Apollos as he said, "It was not at all his desire to come now, but he will come when he has opportunity" (1 Corinthians 16:12). Paul's response reflected the heart of a spiritual leader who realizes he has been called to shepherd and not necessarily be a spiritual dictator.

GOD SPEAKS THROUGH CIRCUMSTANCES

God can open doors that no man can shut (Revelation 3:8). An open door to marriage means that God will clearly speak to both people and give them the freedom to pursue the relationship. Such circumstances need also to be checked by God's Word and godly counsel. An open door to an opportunity for a relationship, a ministry, or a job does not mean that there will not be problems. The apostle Paul spoke of the door that God had opened for him, but in the same verse he mentioned his adversaries (1 Corinthians 16:9).

In some cases we need to "wait on the Lord." In fact when we are not willing to wait, our hearts are probably not in a position of faith. In some cases God allows long delays before He does special things. Such was the case of the birth of Isaac to Abraham and Sarah as well as the birth of John the Baptist to Zacharias and Elizabeth (Romans 4:17–22; Luke 1:5–25, 57–80). A time of waiting can be a vulnerable time but also a rich time for God to do special things in your life.

Since circumstances are certainly open to different interpretations, one needs to be careful to let them be analyzed by godly counsel. We also need to be willing to learn from our past experiences and from times we have been deceived.

KNOWING GOD'S WILL

So how do we know God's will? Can we believe that God has a specific will for each of us and that He is willing to let us in on it? Let's look at a few basic principles.

Believe That God Has a Will for You

When you surrender your life to God, He wants to communicate His will to you. Many people struggle with the fear and tension that they may have missed out on the details of God's itinerary for them and that they are therefore sentenced to His second best. I remember missionary spokesman George Verwer saying if you have missed plan A, there is plan B. If you missed plan B, there is plan C. If you missed plan C, praise God there is a big alphabet.

We should never limit God's power and grace to bring us back to His best. God will work with us where we are, and He can even weave the failures of a person with a repentant heart into something beautiful. God is a God who restores His people. He can even restore the years the locusts have eaten (Joel 2:25). The locusts speak of God's loving discipline in response to the sin of His people.

Be Continually Listening to God

While I was in graduate school I took out a sheet of paper and wrote "future" on the top of it. Every time an idea for the future came into my mind I jotted it down. My ideas might be influenced by the Scriptures, a speaker I heard, a book I was reading, a ministry experience I had, or a conversation with another person. Some ideas would come and go, but over the six years of graduate school the idea of teaching kept coming to the surface. As I reviewed this list, which became quite a few pages long, I found that this theme kept recurring. God confirmed it by the counsel of others and by graciously opening up an opportunity to teach. A call is defined by Oswald Sanders as "a growing conviction as you become acquainted with the facts."

Be Continually Pursuing God

God does have a plan for you. I believe that He has a specific set of good works for each believer (Ephesians 2:10). Our focus should be on the clear guidance of Scripture, and our trust should be in His sovereign will that cannot be thwarted (Ephesians 1:11). We should pursue the completion of His will with the same dependent determination that we see in the apostle Paul and see supremely in Christ. "But I do not consider my life of any account as dear to myself, so that I may finish my course and the ministry which I received from the Lord Jesus, to testify solemnly of the gospel of the grace of God" (Acts 20:24). "Jesus said to them, 'My food is to do the will of Him who sent Me and to accomplish His work'" (John 4:34). "'Father, if You are willing, remove this cup from Me; yet not My will, but Yours be done'" (Luke 22:42).

God's view of success is found in Christ's life and His last words, John 17:4: "I glorified You on the earth, having accomplished the work which You have given Me to do." "Therefore when Jesus had received the sour wine, He said, 'It is finished!' And He bowed His head and gave up His spirit" (John 19:30).

Appeal to God's Glory

God guides us in the paths of righteousness for His name's sake (Psalm 23:3). The psalmist declared, "For Your name's sake You will lead me and guide me" (Psalm 31:3). When a sheep ends up in the right place, no one responds by saying, "What a brilliant sheep!" We have a very gracious, loving, and wise Shepherd. His guidance is usually one step at a time, and our responsibility is to live in an attitude of trusting obedience (Proverbs 3:5–6). Most of us long for a detailed road map as we look for God's guidance. God wants to give us something much better. He desires to give us Himself, an experienced guide. It is better to have an experienced guide than a detailed road map.

Chapter Ten

◆

The Acid Test

Despite the throngs of merry Christmas shoppers at the Borders bookstore, Mary Selkirk sat alone and despondent at her small table near the espresso bar, her neglected coffee growing colder by the minute. Tony, her fiancé—well, almost fiancé—had just left, frustrated at Mary's noncommittal response to his desire to discuss marriage. This wasn't going at all the way Mary thought these things should proceed. The fairy-tale images of a princess and a prince living happily ever after seemed as remote as the moons of Jupiter.

Mary was a dedicated Christian woman. She loved the Lord and was a faithful servant in her church and various mission agencies. She volunteered in the nursery at church. She loved babies, dreaming of the day when she would hold her own infant. She was also thirty-eight years old and unmarried. Most of her friends were long since married, some with high-school-age kids. Time seemed to be running out for her.

She had almost given up on getting married, having gone through a few "sad and bad" relationships with men over the previous two decades. Then she met Tony at work. A rising young salesman in her company, Tony, despite his sometimes brash and aggressive personality, was also a gentleman. After eating dinner together at a trade show in town, Mary discovered that she and Tony had many common interests, including water sports such as scuba diving and water-skiing. Tony made her laugh and treated her like the lady she was, something overlooked by earlier suitors. There was just one problem: Tony wasn't a Christian.

They had talked about religion, but Tony didn't recognize the existence of God or the need for God. Everything in his life was going great. Besides, Tony wasn't about to give up some of his pet interests to become a "monk-like Christian Puritan." Tony liked his drinking, not that he ever became really drunk, but he did like a good drink when he came home after a hard day's work.

Mary was trapped in a dilemma. Normally, these vices of Tony's would be an automatic rejection by Mary. But she loved him despite his vices. And Tony appeared to genuinely love her. He had asked her the previous week to marry him. She hadn't said yes, because of some nagging anxieties within her. She told him that she needed to think things over and talk with her parents about this development. Her parents had met Tony twice and seemed captivated by his charm, though somewhat concerned about his spiritual condition.

Mary went back and forth in her mind, wondering about the relationship and how God might see it. "Is it really such a big deal that Tony drinks? Lots of Christians drink and the Bible doesn't condemn drinking, just drunkenness. After all, God must have put Tony in my life for a reason. I've been praying for someone to share my life with and God has answered that with Tony, hasn't He? Besides, I'm not getting any younger." Mary took a sip of coffee. It was as cold as the falling snow outside the store.

If you were Mary's close friend, what would you tell her to do in order to find God's will in this matter? How should she pray for her situation? Which character attributes of God would it be necessary for Mary to know in order to evaluate the future of the relationship? What Scripture would shed light on her situation? What everyday occurrences or signs should she look for as an answer to her prayers? And how might Satan try to come between her and God?

What immediate decision do you have before you? Is it also a relationship issue, a change of job or vocation, or perhaps a geographical move? Is it a purchase of a home or another major purchase? Is it finding a church or a place of service? Whatever it may be, let's look at the principles from this book that may shed some light on the matter.

If you could ask God a question and get a direct and immediate answer, what would you ask? According to a recent survey the most common response was "What's my purpose here?"[1] God has clearly revealed that His purpose for your life and mine is to build a relationship with Him. It is His desire that we be able to enjoy the fellowship of the One who is perfect in every way. A teenage girl was quoted as saying, "At times I feel I am more committed to godliness than to God." Are you more committed to God's *will* than to *God*? Knowing God is the most basic and fundamental aspect of the will of God for our lives.

In our pursuit of God's will we must also be alert to what we are really pursuing. God has put certain thirsts in our hearts that are a part of our very being. The thirst to feel significant, to have meaning and purpose, and to experience contentment and security are part of all of us. It is very human to attempt to find these needs met in another person, position, or possession. In other words, our pursuit of God's will is always vulnerable to pursuing an idol. We discussed in chapter 4 how these heart thirsts are only completely met as a by-product of trusting, loving, and delighting in God. We all have a spiritual enemy who appeals to our flesh to pursue the road of pride and idolatry.

As you continue to consider the decisions of your life, use them as an opportunity to get to know God. I greatly encourage you to consider the practice I referred to at the end of chapter 1. It involves preparing for the Lord's day by trusting Him with specific things each week and carrying these matters to Him in prayer with an attitude of expectancy. This insight came out of a very dry time in my life and has been extremely helpful.

God is a loving God who delights in working on the matters of our life that concern us (Psalm 138:8). I recall a time a friend told me about taking a homeless man to get a meal. He graciously bought him a nice meal and wanted to talk to him and get to know him. However, after the man ate the meal, he immediately got up and left the restaurant. As my friend reflected on the occasion, he communicated sadly how this reminded him of his own relationship with God. We all too often come to God for our immediate needs, but after they are met, we pursue our independent lives and fail to receive the greater treasure—intimacy with God Himself. The great church leader A. B. Simpson stated his own experience with these words: "Once His gifts I wanted, now the Giver own; Once I sought for blessing, now Himself alone!"

The guidance of God in setting apart Barnabas and Saul for missionary work is recorded in Acts 13:1–3. Guidance came as they were worshiping the Lord. One person has said that worship is the quickening of the conscience by the holiness of God, a feeding of the mind with the truth of God, an opening of the heart to the love of God, and a devoting of the will to the purpose of God. Guidance is a by-product of a worshipful lifestyle.

Lectures in Theology recorded the lectures of a Scottish theologian, John Dick, on the attributes of God. After reading it, I was introduced to Charnack's valuable work *The Existence and Attributes of God.* Packer's *Knowing God* and Tozer's *The Knowledge of the Holy* were also helpful in opening my eyes to the God of the Bible. After writing my doctoral dissertation on "The Attributes of God in Pauline Theology," I studied and lectured on the truths of God's character. I knew it, I believed it, and I even taught about it, but I didn't benefit from the truth of God's character as much as I should have.

I found it a struggle to look at life through the glasses of God's character until I began to take these truths into my prayer closet. I began each day recalling the truth of an attribute and an appropriate application of it for that day. This was so helpful that I've encouraged hundreds of other people to do the same—to find some way to review the truth of God's character that aids in worship. You can write the characteristics of God on 3 x 5 cards with key verses and key applications, one card for each attribute. Then review one or two cards a day and continually keep this truth before you. You might start by looking at the truths of God in chapters 5–8 of this book. Let your pursuit of worship be the primary way in which you pursue His will.

A number of years ago I ran across one of Norman Grubb's books entitled *Touching the Invisible.* One of the chapters of this book is entitled "How We Obtained Guidance." He related the method his mission board used to get direction from God. After spiritually preparing themselves to ascertain that they were submitted to Him and that their objective was God's glory, they diligently gathered all the facts they could that might aid them in their decision. After thoroughly examining the situation and the Scriptures that threw light on it, they then waited on the Lord for His confirmation. He writes:

> So in order to know His voice, we now change the tactics. We have been occupied in thinking over our problem, but now we deliberately cease to think about it. When God speaks, He always speaks in stillness. While our hearts are disturbed and our minds busy on a situation, His voice cannot be heard. Our inward attitude must be like a pool of water. If disturbed, no reflection can be seen in it. When still, the features can be seen. So the best thing we can do, having stored our minds with the facts, is to leave them with God. It is not a state of forgetfulness, but a redirection of our attention. We were concentrated on the problem; now we concentrate on Him, the Solver.[2]

On one occasion during my senior year in college I had been on a diligent pursuit of God's next step for my life. I had majored in business at Auburn University, and God had graciously blessed my studies. I had considered pursuing an MBA and had conferred with two fine Christian men who had done their MBAs at Harvard University and were presently working for Campus

Crusade for Christ. I would go to the library and look at the Harvard catalogue. I was also considering interviewing with some companies that were coming to campus. Another option was going immediately into a Christian ministry, and the fourth option was going to seminary to do graduate work in theology.

I wrote a prayer letter and sent it to many people, asking them to pray for this decision. I also diligently sought godly counsel and collected many catalogues of graduate schools in theology. God used this lengthy process of evaluating these options to confirm His call to pursue vocational ministry. In fact, a businessman who had shown a great deal of interest in my working with his company one day said, "We have people like you working for our company who want to get off work to do what they really want to do." A valuable work on the subject of God's call to ministry is the first chapter to Spurgeon's book *Lectures to my Students,* which God used to confirm His direction for me. As a result I decided not to interview with the companies that were coming to campus.

I also eliminated the option of the MBA from Harvard. While my idea was to use the training in the area of Christian service, I always had a strong reserve from the Spirit every time I looked at the Harvard catalogue. I can now clearly see that this business training was not in line with my primary spiritual gifts of teaching and exhorting.

My deep desire to go right into the ministry was met with strong counsel to get training first. This counsel came from my parents as well as older, wiser men in the ministry. I did not like this advice at all at first. However, in time it became my desire.

As I continued to talk and pray with various ones about where I should go, I sensed God's Spirit convicting me of my anxiety. It was as if I was praying in a spirit of unbelief. When I began praising God that He would clearly lead me, my mind began to be focused on the Solver and not the problem. The very next day I talked with a godly pastor who was providentially in my path. He had studied at Dallas Theological Seminary, and our conversation confirmed I was to take a step of faith in that direction. Dallas would be the place where I would spend the next six years of my life.

God faithfully confirms time and time again that He is a God who desires to communicate His will. His primary means of communication is His Word. Try beginning the practice of meditation on His Word when you're fearful. I was asked to do a national radio program one evening a number of years ago. It was a call-in show on which I would be asked various Bible questions. I agreed to pray about it. My fear was, "What if I get a question I can't answer? The whole world will see my ignorance." Then I read Psalm 67:7, "God blesses us, that all the ends of the earth may fear Him." God used the principle of Psalm 67:7 to give assurance to my spirit, I took the step of faith, and God mercifully blessed. We are to seek the Lord at every point of fear (Psalm 34:4) and let His Word be used of Him to love us at our point of fear (1 John 4:18). In gray areas where you need discernment whether it is right or wrong for you to do something, you can review the nine questions on pages 160–61.

God's will is not a decision that we are to pursue alone. We need the collective wisdom of God's people. I'm grateful for the time my mother counseled me not to pursue a relationship with a young lady; that was God's way of leading me eventually to the person He had for me to marry in His timing. I believe that Mary in our opening story also is grateful for the godly counsel she received not to pursue marriage to Tony.

One key aspect of the will of God is genuine submission to God. I remember walking to the train with a former marine one day. He described how he had learned more about submitting to authority from living with his mother than from his experience in the marines. He said, "When my mother said to jump she wanted me to be asking, 'How high?' on the way up." George Mueller stated that 90 percent of the problems in regard to the will of God are related to not being truly submissive to God. Let us heed the wise counsel of the German reformer Martin Luther, who stated, "I have held many things in my hands, and have lost them all; but whatever I have placed in God's hand, that I still possess."

Submission does not mean that you don't desire what God's will entails. The revelation of the character of God is designed to win your heart to Him and His will. His will does not mean that you pursue every ministry that has a need. As Henrietta Mears said, "A need does not constitute a call." Richard Foster wisely said, "To say yes to an opportunity might be saying no to a commitment."

Look at the six points that Mueller outlined in regard to his own pursuit of God's will.

SIX STEPS TO KNOWING GOD'S WILL

1. I seek at the beginning to get my heart into such a state that it has no will of its own in regard to a given matter. Nine-tenths of the trouble with people is just here. Nine-tenths of the difficulties are overcome when our hearts are ready to do the Lord's will, whatever it may be. When one is truly in this state, it is usually but a little way to the knowledge of what His will is.

2. Having done this, I do not leave the result to feeling or simple impression. If I do so, I make myself liable to great delusions.

3. I see the will of the Spirit of God through, or in connection with, the Word of God. The Spirit and the Word must be combined. If I look to the Spirit alone without the Word, I lay myself open to great delusions also. If the Holy Spirit guides us at all, He will do it according to the Scriptures and never contrary to them.

4. Next I take into account providential circumstances. These often plainly indicate God's will in connection with His Word and Spirit.

5. I ask God in prayer to reveal His will to me aright.

6. Thus, through prayer to God, the study of the Word, and reflection, I come to a deliberate judgment according to the best of my ability and knowledge; and if my mind is thus at peace, and continues so after two or three more petitions, I proceed accordingly. In trivial matters, and in transactions involving more important issues, I have found this method always effective.

The last step calls for a decision of faith. God honors decisions of faith and the use of sanctified common sense. One friend of mine chose his career based on the premise that it would give him more time to spend with his family. His starting salary after graduation with an MBA from the University of Chicago was not great, but he has been rewarded financially since then. Although it may be possible to make too much of human reason, it is also possible to make too little of it. Remember that a Christian is God's servant and is to live for God's glory. A servant has the right to know the orders of His loving Master, and God desires to glorify Himself through you as you seek His will.

The pursuit of God's will is first and foremost a pursuit of God Himself. To seek God's will and not God will result in confusion. All our efforts at seeking God are only a response to His working in our life. God saved Augustine of Hippo, a great church leader of the fourth century, out of a life of great shame. He also placed in him a passion for Himself that led to a life of great usefulness. May Augustine's prayer be your own: "O Lord, grant that I may desire Thee, and desiring Thee, seek Thee, and seeking Thee, find Thee, and finding Thee, be satisfied with Thee forever."

NOTES

1. Pastor's Weekly Briefing, 10 September 1999, 2.
2. Norman Grubb, *Touching the Invisible* (Fort Washington, Pa.: Christian Literature Crusade, 1980), 25.

NOTE: To reflect on what we have explored so far, go to the personal journal on page 196.

Personal Journal Entries Reflecting on Sections One Through Four

Journal Entry for Section One. At some point in their lives, everyone comes to ask himself or herself about the meaning of one's own purpose. "Why am I here?" or "What does God intend for me to do?" are common questions. Knowing what you do now after having read Section One, record your thoughts about God's purpose for your life. Did you always think this way? With which of the six symptoms of Satan's tactics discussed in chapter 2 can you most readily identify?

Chapter ①

Write ③ Concerns to take to
Him Sunday morning.
Purpose for redemption:
① Relationship with Him
② Service to Him

Journal Entry for Section Two. Knowing God is essential to discerning His will for your life. In your journal, write down what comes to your mind when you think of God. After you have recorded your thoughts, review your words in light of the following ideas: (1) Do you sense His delight in you, and do you delight in Him? (2) What area of your life is the hardest to trust Him as you examine the three evidences of faith in chapter 3? Write down your reflections on the four aspects of God's will for you in chapter 4. Which is the greatest struggle—right view of self, meaning and purpose, contentment, or security?

_____

_____

_____

_____

_____

_____

_____

_____

_____

_____

_____

_____

_____

_____

_____

_____

_____

_____

_____

_____

_____

_____

_____

_____

_____

_____

_____

_____

_____

_____

_____

_____

_____

_____

_____

_____

_____

_____

_____

Journal Entry for Section Three. Write down a major decision that you need to make. Take time to worship God based on the truths that you find in chapters 5 through 8. Write down any guidance that you discover.

_____

_____

_____

_____

_____

_____

_____

_____

_____

_____

_____

_____

_____

_____

_____

_____

_____

_____

_____

_____

_____

_____

_____

_____

_____

_____

_____

_____

_____

_____

_____

_____

_____

_____

_____

_____

_____

_____

_____

_____

_____

_____

_____

Journal Entry for Section Four. Thinking back to a past event, record how you saw (or now see) God working in fulfilling His will in your life. It might either be a time when you acted upon His prompting or ignored God to do things your own way. What did God communicate to you through Scripture, the prompting of His Spirit, circumstances, and other people? What is your plan for making meditation of Scripture a part of your life?

_____

_____

_____

_____

_____

_____

_____

_____

_____

_____

_____

_____

_____

_____

_____

_____

Journal Entry for Your Life Today. Record a current issue in your life for which you need God's guidance. How are you responding to this issue? What are your prayers? What should you be looking for as an answer to your prayers and questions? How will knowing God help direct your prayers? What resources can you use to better know His will for you?

_____

_____

_____

_____

_____

_____

_____

_____

_____

_____

_____

_____

_____

_____

_____

_____

_____

Moody Press, a ministry of Moody Bible Institute,
is designed for education, evangelization, and edification.
If we may assist you in knowing more about Christ
and the Christian life, please write us without obligation:
Moody Press, c/o MLM, Chicago, IL 60610.